# AAAS Selected Symposia Series

Published by Westview Press, Inc.
5500 Central Avenue, Boulder, Colorado

for the

American Association for the Advancement of Science
1776 Massachusetts Ave., N.W., Washington, D.C.

# The Environmental Effects of Nuclear War

*Edited by Julius London and Gilbert F. White*

*AAAS Selected* **98**

AAAS Selected Symposia Series

Copyright © 1984 by the American Association for the Advancement of Science

Published in 1984 in the United States of America by
    Westview Press, Inc.
    5500 Central Avenue
    Boulder, Colorado 80301
    Frederick A. Praeger, Publisher

Library of Congress Cataloging in Publication Data
Main entry under title:
The Environmental effects of nuclear war.
(A Westview replica edition)
Bibliography: p.
1. Atomic warfare--Environmental aspects. I. London, Julius, 1917-
II. White, Gilbert Fowler, 1911-   .
U263.E58 1984          363.3'498          84-19699
ISBN 0-8133-7014-0

Printed and bound in the United States of America

10 9 8 7 6 5 4 3 2 1

# About the Book

This book assesses the current available information concerning the major scientific problems related to environmental consequences of a possible nuclear war. The contributors address a broad range of topics, among them the effects of blast, heat, and local radioactive fallout; the likely dispersal patterns and residence times of radioactive debris in the troposphere and stratosphere; the probable long-term effects on both the local and global biosphere and radiological consequences for humans; the effect on the global environment of widespread fires in urban and industrialized regions; and the likely significant decrease of stratospheric ozone with a resulting long-term increase in harmful UV radiation received at the ground.

The authors point to problem areas where current information is inadequate or completely lacking and discuss the role of the scientist in developing such information as a contribution to the elimination of the nuclear war threat.

# About the Series

The *AAAS Selected Symposia Series* was begun in 1977 to
provide a means for more permanently recording and more
widely disseminating some of the valuable material which is
discussed at the AAAS Annual National Meetings.  The volumes
in this *Series* are based on symposia held at the Meetings
which address topics of current and continuing significance,
both within and among the sciences, and in the areas in which
science and technology impact on public policy.  The *Series*
format is designed to provide for rapid dissemination of
information, so the papers are not typeset but are reproduced
directly from the camera-copy submitted by the authors.  The
papers are organized and edited by the symposium arrangers
who then become the editors of the various volumes.  Most
papers published in this *Series* are original contributions
which have not been previously published, although in some
cases additional papers from other sources have been added
by an editor to provide a more comprehensive view of a
particular topic.  Symposia may be reports of new research
or reviews of established work, particularly work of an
interdisciplinary nature, since the AAAS Annual Meetings
typically embrace the full range of the sciences and their
societal implications.

WILLIAM D. CAREY
*Executive Officer*
*American Association for*
*the Advancement of Science*

# Contents

# Tables and Figures

# 1. The Environmental Effects of Nuclear War—An Overview

## Introduction

Until recent years the evaluation of nuclear warfare effects has been chiefly in terms of the direct impacts of the blast, heat and local radioactive fallout as they destroy humans, artifacts and social structure. Much of the public debate over the notions of a winnable, limited nuclear war and of survival thereafter has focused on the enormity of demands placed upon medical assistance for those people who live through the initial blast, the rationale or absurdity of plans to carry out massive evacuations as a means of deterring or mitigating the consequences of nuclear attacks, and the complexity of reconstruction.

Now, greater attention is turning toward the environmental consequences of nuclear detonations. This is basically because of increasing recognition that regardless of the immediate impact on lives, health, buildings, public facilities and the means of production, nuclear explosions might drastically alter if not, perhaps, fatally impair the life support systems of the globe. The vision of increasing through civil defense the number of survivors from direct impacts becomes morbidly whimsical if the survivors are in environments no longer capable of providing essential water and food.

It is now generally believed that there is no tenable concept of a winnable nuclear war. Most observers agree that once a nuclear exchange

1

is started it would most likely quickly escalate to a "total" war. Whether or not they are correct could only be proven by an initially limited nuclear exchange that might or might not trigger a broader, cataclysmic conflict. It has, however, become clear that the consequences of a mass nuclear exchange, if it were to occur, would be so catastrophic that all efforts must be exercised to prevent it. What are these consequences?

The following papers review recent efforts towards providing information on the short and long-term environmental consequences of total nuclear war. They do not deal with social or economic disruption to normal functions of society, nor with psychological trauma that may be caused by the extreme events, nor the breakdown of medical and other emergency support systems, topics which are nevertheless of profound importance in consideration of global consequences of such a calamitous event (see, for instance, Chazov and Vartanian, 1982; Laulan, 1982).

In the case of a widespread nuclear exchange as envisaged by some analysts, the intermediate and long-term effects would not necessarily be contained within any specific geographic area. In those circumstances the concept of a battlefield would no longer be applicable even if it were possible to limit the exchange to so-called tactical weapons. The use of tactical or counterforce targets would, in the view of those analysts, quickly extend to attacks on other than purely military nuclear installations.

The quality and extent of impairment to widespread life support systems from various patterns of nuclear explosions have been in controversy. Some sanguine observers have predicted that populations remote from direct bomb produced effects of light, heat and explosive blasts, and adequately protected from short-term fallout, would survive those early threats to life and health and promptly could set about the task of reconstructing their damaged physical and social systems. At the other extreme, observers have asserted that the impacts of a major exchange of nuclear warheads would wound the environment sufficiently to render the globe unable to support any substantial human population beyond a period of months or years. In between, and depending in part on assumptions made as to the number and nature of the detonations, are a variety of estimates as to the scope of environmental effects.

A number of comprehensive reviews of the contamination resulting from nuclear fallout were published in the 1960s and 1970s (e.g. Annenkov et al., 1973; Bensen and Sparrow, 1971; Glasstone and Dolan, 1977; Polikarpov, 1966; Woodwell and Whittaker, 1968). As the official view of nuclear arms as a basis for massive deterrence shifted to entertain the possibility of limited nuclear exchanges and of rebuilding a viable society thereafter, public discussions of environment effects received less attention. Relatively few new reports on research findings appeared until 1982. Contemplation of nuclear destruction in the here and now was apparently accompanied in some government quarters by reluctance to discuss or look into its meaning for the future of human welfare.

## Aims of the Symposium

In 1981, members of section W, Meteorology and Hydrology, of the American Association for the Advancement of Science, forwarded a resolution to the AAAS Council which was subsequently passed by the Council. The resolution, A Catastrophe of Thermonuclear War, stated, in part, "Whereas there is a worldwide anxiety of the possibility of large scale nuclear warfare, and whereas recent studies have shown that nuclear warfare would inevitably cause death, disease and human suffering of epidemic proportion without any medical intervention possible, and whereas severe trauma to biological and ecological systems would be extended far beyond the immediate bomb impact areas by virtue of transport of lethal radioactive debris by air and water, . . . therefore be it resolved that the Council of the AAAS support national and international efforts directed towards the prevention of nuclear war, and be it further resolved that a symposium be held at the next annual meeting on the general subject of The Effects of Thermonuclear War."[1]

The symposium was held on 28 May 1983 as part of the annual AAAS meeting in Detroit, Michigan.

---

[1] The full text of this resolution adopted on 7 January 1982 is given in Appendix A.

The present volume contains the papers, edited slightly, presented at that symposium.

The major aim of the symposium papers was to review the current state of knowledge and ignorance on these matters. While the known environmental effects were to be specified, gaps in information and understanding were to be recognized and questions especially deserving of answers through research were to be identified. It was clear from the beginning that discussion of the likely catastrophic consequences of a nuclear war did not imply that such an event is inevitable, nor did it contemplate that these consequences could be significantly modified and reduced as a result of judicious selection of types of weapons or the pattern of deployment. The symposium participants, as a group, represent broad scientific interests in the subject matter of the current discussion and each has particular expertise in specific areas of concern dealing with environmental effects of nuclear bomb explosions.

Although the papers in this volume are directed primarily at impacts on a global scale, they indicate here and there specific local effects. It is notable that there have been only a few efforts to estimate these consequences in the concrete and constrained dimensions of a single community. Some estimates have been made of the direct impacts of an explosion on people and structures, as witness the many "ground zero" exercises, and the reports from the Office of Technology Assessment, the Physicians for Social Responsibility, and the World Health Organization. However, studies for specific ecosystems at the local level have only begun to be carried out (e.g., Bennett et al., 1984).

## Parallel Efforts

After or while the symposium was planned, a series of initiatives along similar lines were mounted. Among the principal ones were:

The Scientific Committee on Problems of the Environment (SCOPE), under the auspices of the International Council of Scientific Unions, organized an international, interdisciplinary review of the state of knowledge of environmental effects of nuclear detonations, involving representatives of

4

national academies of science and international scientific unions (this is
described in chapter 8);

The United Nations Environment Programme
funded the Stockholm International
Peace Research Institute to undertake a
five-year program of study and inter-
pretation on military activities, including nuclear war, in relation to the
environment;

The Rockefeller Family Fund with the Kendall
Foundation and associated funding agencies organized a conference on the Long-
Term Worldwide Biological Consequences of
Nuclear War, held in Washington, D.C. on
31 October - 1 November 1983; and leading
to two major publications (Turco et al.,
1983; Ehrlich et al., 1983);

U.S. National Academy of Sciences (at the
request of the Department of Defense)
launched a study of atmospheric effects
of nuclear war to be published in 1984;
and

The Ecological Society of America authorized
a review to be completed in mid-1984, of
ecosystem impacts of nuclear detonation.

The papers presented at the symposium were
prepared against the background of earlier research and research reviews that had begun in the
1950s. As recorded in the lists of cited refer-
ences, those previous studies, principally in the
U.S. and the USSR, had provided the basis for a
number of relatively comprehensive reviews.
Notable were the National Academy of Sciences
study of 1975, the Congressional Office of Technology Assessment review of 1979, Ambio volume XI,
1982, and the World Health Organization report of
1983. In addition, there had been a major wave of
semi-popular literature in which Jonathan Schell's
The Fate of the Earth (1982) was most prominent.

## Variables of a Nuclear War Scenario

In this volume, as in comparable analyses,
the specification of the nuclear detonations is
useful to what follows, and requires some assumptions as to the chief variables either in
terms of scenarios or of parameters. The chief
variables clearly are: energy released, composition of the bomb, height of the burst, location
and number of detonations, season, time of day,

5

and large scale weather patterns during the time of the most intense bomb explosions. When the range of possible combinations of different values of these variables is taken into account it is apparent that the number is immense. Although it is not possible to state precisely what, where, and when will be the pattern of the weapons used in a possible nuclear exchange, some things can be said, within useful bounds, about the significant variables that need to be considered for a pertinent discussion.

In an all-out nuclear war, it is generally assumed that approximately 15,000-20,000 warheads of various types might be used each with equivalent energy range of approximately a few hundred tons (tactical weapons) to ten megatons (Mt) (of TNT equivalent), and an average yield per bomb of about 500 kilotons (roughly about the equivalent energy involved in the Mount St. Helens eruption, 18 May 1980) (see, for instance, Newell and Deepak, 1980). The total yield could thus be about 10,000 Mt (of the order of 1 million Hiroshima bombs). The Ambio scenario postulated this yield level, and the analysis by Turco et al., (1983) examined a much wider range of yields, from 100 Mt to 25,000 Mt in different circumstances.

The immediate targets would probably be military installations, industrial and urban centers, and refineries, in the U.S. and Europe. Thus, the major targets would probably be concentrated in mid-latitudes of the Northern Hemisphere. Some analysts speculate that perhaps 10 percent of the initial explosions would be over ocean areas or in the Southern Hemisphere. It should be emphasized that although the specific targets are of great importance in evaluating the immediate impact of such a nuclear exchange, they become less significant when considering intermediate and long-term effects. The height of detonation would probably be divided between ground and air bursts -- with most of the military targets being subjected to ground bursts and industrial targets subjected to air bursts. The short and long-term effects would depend significantly on the height of deployment and equivalent yield of the bombs.

In general, the lower the burst level, the lower would be the casualties from blast effects and thermal radiation, but the higher would be the casualties from local radioactive fallout. A low-level explosion has a close-in early fallout pattern, extending out to the order of one to a few hundred kilometers, over a period of up to 24 hours. High level blasts, particularly those reaching up into the stratosphere, have much longer fallout periods, months to years, with a larger hemispheric or global area affected (Kellogg et al., 1957).

It is also not possible to predict the season during which bombing operations might start. This is quite important for immediate and intermediate (short-term) effects, but of less importance for long-term effects. During the winter the atmospheric circulation is stronger than during the summer and more variable, both in the troposphere and stratosphere. During the summer the circulation is westerly in the troposphere (relatively weak) and easterly in the stratosphere. These differences give rise to differences in large scale transport of radioactive debris. Since the height of the nuclear cloud is a function of the yield, the seasonal influence would be different for different bomb strengths. Of course, on any particular day, the wind pattern can be highly variable at any particular place and from location to location.

Other meteorological conditions would strongly affect the vertical spreading of the resultant radioactive debris and would depend on the general vertical thermal stability of the troposphere. Because of the relatively low level of the tropopause at high latitudes, nuclear clouds resulting from bomb explosions at subpolar latitudes during winter would penetrate more easily into the stratosphere than clouds from similar bursts in the tropics. In addition, because the smaller radioactive particles can act as cloud condensation nuclei, the fallout pattern, after the first few days following the nuclear explosions, would follow the large scale precipitation distribution.

For many reasons it is convenient to consider the types of effects to be expected as a result of nuclear bomb explosions in terms of different effective time and space scales. These extend from immediate (direct) to long-term (years), and

7

from the close-in blast area to global scales. The most extensive background discussion, currently available, of the different types of effects to be expected is that contained in Glasstone and Dolan (1977). A schematic diagram of the major effects is given in Fig. 1-1. The specialized terms used in the diagram and in the following discussions are defined in the abbreviated glossary at the end of this volume.

The energy released at the instant of a nuclear bomb burst of equivalent yield of one megaton is about $4.2 \times 10^{15}$ joules. Within about one microsecond the temperature is increased to tens of millions of degrees and the bomb becomes a cauldron of nuclear, chemical, and thermodynamic processes. The immediate effects of the nuclear explosions involve a sudden high pressure (blast) wave, thermal radiation, and ionizing radiation associated with the bomb detonation. The impact of these effects are felt within the first few seconds to hours after the explosion. Considering the total energy released by a nuclear weapon, on the average about 50 percent is released as a blast wave, 40 percent is released as a thermal wave, and 10 percent is released as ionizing radiation.

The blast wave is caused by the tremendous sudden increase of pressure, to over a million atmospheres, as the bomb material vaporizes and expands as a result of the extremely high temperature. The subsequent blast effects depend on the height of the detonation. For a near surface explosion, there would be severe cratering with large quantities of soil material sucked up in the nuclear cloud, and maximum fallout within a few hundred kilometers of the explosion. For a bomb burst with an equivalent yield of 1 Mt the resulting blast would create a pressure wave, traveling initially at supersonic speeds, about one-third in excess of atmospheric pressure at a distance of about 5 kilometers. This is equivalent to a wall of water over 3 meters high moving outward at excessively high speeds and would completely destroy most structures over an area of about 25 square kilometers. At a distance of 5 kilometers from the explosion, the winds caused by this severe overpressure would be stronger than 250 km hr$^{-1}$ (tornado strength), resulting in a significant fraction of deaths among the human and animal population in the area, and the destruction of trees and vegetation.

For a bomb burst at a height of 2.5 kilometers, there would be severe lethal damage and property destruction covering an area in excess of 100 square kilometers. Of course, most of the blast deaths in this area would be the result of collapsed buildings and flying debris. The blast effects would also cause extensive earth slides in rough terrain and would rupture electric circuits and gas or oil lines thus increasing the danger of widespread fires.

The high temperature at the center of a nuclear bomb cloud immediately after an explosion results in an abrupt enhanced thermal radiation over the whole electromagnetic spectrum. The resulting increased ultraviolet, visible and near infrared radiation could be responsible for extensive retinal damage and second and third degree burns out to a distance of ten to fifteen kilometers. In addition, the intense heat wave would most assuredly start numerous fires igniting structures, and varied types of combustible materials, including vegetation and forests, over an area 100-200 square kilometers.

The lethal range from direct nuclear radiation following the explosion of a one megaton device is about 5 kilometers from the point of explosion. However, about 50 percent of the radioactive bomb material and earth debris comes down within a few days as local fallout within a distance of a few hundred kilometers of the detonation, depending on the local winds. For a single explosion, the local lethal fallout for humans, animals, and most vegetation could cover an area of over 1000 square kilometers. With increased yield and height of the bomb burst, the delay time and area covered by the fallout is increased, thus allowing for the ingestion of radioactive substances which enter the food chain and reach sensitive body organs after being deposited on plants, soil, or water.

The short-term lethal damage to the human and animal population from the combined effects of blast, heat, and radiation would extend out to a distance of about 60 kilometers.

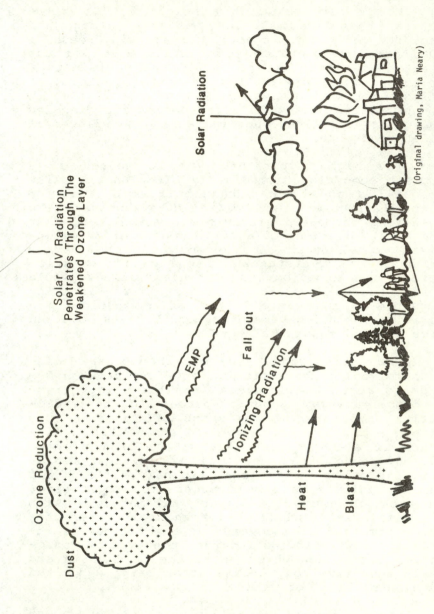

Fig. 1-1. Schematic diagram of the major effects of nuclear bomb explosions.

High altitude bomb bursts produce an electromagnetic wave of extremely short pulse (EMP) that
creates an electric signal similar to that associated with lightning but of much shorter duration.
Although such a pulse does not represent any
direct physical threat to humans, it could if, for
instance, exploded over central Kansas, disable
the electric power and communication network over
a significant portion of the U.S.

When human and environmental consequences of
a nuclear war are extrapolated beyond the immediate effects of a single bomb detonation additional
concerns become paramount. As discussed by Dr.
Herbert Abrams in his testimony before the Gore
U.S. Congressional sub-committee investigating the
Consequences of Nuclear War on the Global Environment (see U.S. Congress, 1982), many of these
concerns involve the extensive outbreak of infection and the spread of disease among human and
animal survivors of the initial attacks.

Radiation effects significantly weaken the
body immune system which would be aggravated by
malnutrition resulting from decreased food supply
and disruption of the normal food distribution
channels. The spread of disease is accelerated
by the disruption of normal sanitation facilities
and the dramatic increase of the insect population. These problems are made more serious by
the expected high number of casualties of medical
personnel and facilities normally concentrated in
large urban areas (Abrams and Von Kaenel, 1981).
Over a period of years there would certainly be an
increased incidence of radiation induced cancers
and genetic disorders.

The Hiroshima and Nagasaki experience shows
the devastating effects from local fires set off
by those miniature (according to present capability) nuclear explosions. In addition to local destruction, however, the long-term global consequence involving climatic and biospheric effects
could be horrendous to any surviving population,
as has been shown by recent investigations. It
was recently estimated in a study conducted under
the auspices of the World Health Organization that
such a war ". . . would result in about
1,150,000,000 dead and 1,100,000,000 people injured. Altogether, about half of the world's pop-

ulation would be immediate victims of the war." (World Health Organization, 1983).

Multi-detonations, as envisaged in any nuclear war scenario would be responsible for widespread smoke and dust clouds as a result of fires ignited in urban and industrial centers, forests and croplands, gas and oil fields. These smoke and dust clouds would extend into the upper troposphere and lower stratosphere and be spread out over a large portion of the Northern Hemisphere and possibly portions of the Southern Hemisphere (Pittock, 1982). Because the cloud particles have a high optical depth in the visible, the solar irradiance at the earth's surface in the Northern Hemisphere could be reduced to a few percent of its normal value over a period of a couple of weeks or so. During this time if such reductions occurred the temperature over continental areas in mid-latitudes of the Northern Hemisphere could drop by about 40° C with subfreezing temperatures lasting for several months as first pointed out by Crutzen and Birks (1982) (see, also, Turco et al., 1983). Although this cooling might be mitigated somewhat by the increased concentration of tropospheric smog and an enhanced delayed greenhouse effect some months after the explosions, the synergistic effects of reduced sunlight, lowered surface temperature, and radioactive fallout over large areas and for extended periods of time would result in severe trauma to the earth's biological support system with a consequent precipitous reduction in the world's food supply (Ehrlich et al., 1983).

## Topics and Authors

While there was attraction for the symposium organizers in the notion of adopting a particular combination of variables embodied in a single "scenario" it seemed unwise to do so at that stage of investigation. To fix on one combination, such as in the Ambio scenario, would gain specificity but would exclude consideration of many other possible sets of events, and would hamper imaginative canvass of consequences. Investigators had the choice of specifying a particular scenario or scenarios by selecting a set of reasonable assumptions, or of analyzing the possible effects of varying individual parameters according to their best judgment. No attempt was made to rigidly require either method, and it was recognized that the authors would have had little patience with such restraints.

Underlying this or any similar review is an ethical concern. Any systematic exploration of the subject raises the twin questions of: (1) Does such examination give credibility to the expectation that nuclear weapons at some time will be used on a large scale? (2) Does any effort to quantify the effects of weapons on life support systems suggest that the analyst is providing a basis for estimating some maximum limit of explosions which might be tolerated short of utter destruction of those systems as, for instance, a battle strategy involving precise and discriminating targeting restricted to military installations even in the unlikely event that this was possible? An appropriate response to these questions was given by Draper (1984):

> There is no necessary moral choice between the admittedly terrible slaughter of a limited, controlled nuclear war and the possible mutual annihilation of an all-out nuclear war, and even less if the terrible slaughter may well end up in mutual annihilation. If morality enters at all, it is in how to avoid such a choice, not in how to make it.

It is important to treat these issues in the context of views among scientists as reported in chapter 8.

As a base on which other estimates of effects may build, we begin in chapter 2 with the calculations of Duffield and von Hippel of human casualties from blast, thermal radiation, and short-term fallout for three cases of nuclear weapon use. These are the effects most often assessed in connection with postulated nuclear attack. Their analysis shows that serious questions can be raised as to the realism of the estimates that have been published by the Department of Energy for such events. It also reminds the reader that beyond those direct impacts there may be large and complex effects resulting from impairment of the physical, biological, and social environments. The four following chapters suggest what those may be.

13

However, we do not attempt to specify or quantify the consequences of human suffering from social disorganization and destruction of artifacts from the bursts. The problems of medical services, housing, food, transport, industrial production, and all other aspects of recovery from bombing as outlined by Katz (1982), the World Health Organization (1983), and others are excluded. We begin instead with a description of the immediate destruction that would result from a nuclear exchange and then focus on the environmental consequences and ethical concerns of scientists in preventing such an exchange.

We have also omitted any discussions of policy decisions involving nuclear strategy, a subject of considerable current debate (see, for instance, Wieseltier, 1983).

The immediate short-term destructive effects of combat scale nuclear weapon explosions on civilian populations and structures are summarized by Frank von Hippel, professor of public and international affairs, Center for Energy and Environmental Studies, Princeton University, and John Duffield, research assistant at the Center. Lester Machta, Director of the Air Resources Laboratory (NOAA) describes the results of studies on the transport and atmospheric residence times of airborne radioactive material resulting from simulated and actual bomb tests in the 1950s. The extremely high temperature associated with nuclear explosions is responsible for massive production of oxides of nitrogen which, if present in the stratosphere, would significantly reduce the total atmospheric ozone content. This would result in increasing the ultraviolet radiation received at the ground to the extent of causing an alarming increase of skin cancer and producing severe trauma to the entire ecosystem (National Academy of Sciences, 1982). This topic is discussed by Julius Chang, formerly deputy division leader of the Theoretical Physics Division at Lawrence Livermore National Laboratory and currently program director of the Acid Rain Project at NCAR, and Donald Wuebbles, physicist at Lawrence Livermore National Laboratory.

Certainly one of the truly alarming long-term effects to be considered is that involving radiation contamination of humans, including the strong

14

potential for carcinogetic and potential genetic effects. Arthur Upton, Director of the Institute of Environmental Medicine at New York University, draws from his analysis of the information on the effects of human population due to exposure to ionizing radiation, to summarize the available results.

Much of the discussion in the literature of the results of a mass nuclear bomb exchange deals with the effects immediately following the bombing operations. The long-term consequences for plants and animals involve, in addition to observed contamination effects, widespread fires from the burning of cities, forests, and crops which could produce a canopy of smoke that would prevent most of the sun's radiation from reaching the ground over the severely affected areas. Such contamination and severe extinction of solar energy with their calamitous injury to both natural and managed ecosystems is the subject of the paper by George Woodwell, Director of the Ecosystems Study Center at the Marine Biological Laboratory at Woods Hole.

There are many uncertainties in the evaluation of the full scale of significant environmental consequences of nuclear war. These uncertainties need to be identified and problem areas for vigorous research efforts need to be defined. A discussion of these uncertainties and problems is covered in the chapter written by the editors.

The final paper deals with the role of the scientist who is concerned with environmental consequences of nuclear war as discussed in the previous chapters and who is sensitive to the social and ethical responsibilities that relate to that scientific knowledge and competence. This problem is addresses by Thomas Malone from his background of experience in the atmospheric sciences and in the organization of scientific cooperation at the international scale.

Those who joined in the symposium did so in the conviction that by illuminating some of the consequences of the use of nuclear weaponry they could temper the political disposition to treat it seriously as a possible instrument of international policy.

15

# References

Abrams, H. L. and W. E. Von Kaenel, 1981: Medical problems of survivors of nuclear war, N. E. J. of Med., 305, 1226-1232.

Annenkov, B. N., I. K. Dibobes, and R. M. Aleksakin, eds., 1973: Radiobiology and Radioecology of Farm Animals, U.S. Atomic Energy Commission Technical Information Center, Oak Ridge, TN.

Bennett, J. O., P. S. C. Johnson, J. R. Key, D. C. Pattie and A. H. Taylor, 1984: Foreseeable effects of nuclear detonations on a local environment: Boulder County, Colorado, Environmental Conservation, 11, 155-156.

Benson, D. and A. Sparrow, eds., 1971: Survival of Food Crops and Livestock in the Event of Nuclear War, U.S. Atomic Energy Commission, Washington, D.C.

Chazov, E. I. and M. E. Vartanian, 1982: Effects of human behavior, Ambio XI, 158-160.

Crutzen, P. J., and J. W. Birks, 1982: The atmosphere after a nuclear war: twilight at noon, Ambio, XI, 114-125.

Draper, T., 1984: Nuclear Temptation, New York Review, January 19, 42-50.

Ehrlich, P. R., J. Harte, M. A. Harwell, P. H. Raven, C. Sagan, G. M. Woodwell, J. Berry, E. S. Ayensu, A. H. Ehrlich, T. Eisner, S. J. Gould, H. D. Grover, R. Herrera, R. M. May, E. Mayr, C. P. McKay, H. A. Mooney, N. Myers, D. Pimentel, J. M. Teal, 1983: Long-term biological consequences of nuclear war, Science, 222, 1293-1300.

Glasstone, S., and P. J. Dolan, eds., 1977: The Effects of Nuclear Weapons, 3rd ed., U. S. Dept. of Def. and the Energy Res. and Dev. Adm. Washington, D.C.

Katz, A. M., 1982: Life After Nuclear War - The Economic and Social Impacts of Nuclear Attacks on the United States, Ballinger, New York.

Kellogg, W. W., R. R. Rapp, and S. M. Greenfield, 1957: Close-in fallout, J. Meteo., 14, 1-8.

Laulan, Y., 1982: The economic consequences: back to the dark ages, Ambio, XI, 149-152.

National Academy of Sciences, 1982: Causes and Effects of Stratospheric Ozone Reduction: An Update, National Academy of Sciences Press, Washington, D.C.

Newell, R. E., and A. Deepak, eds., 1982: Mount
    St. Helens Eruptions of 1980, NASA, SP-458,
    Scientific and Technical Information.
Pittock, A. B., 1982: Nuclear Explosions and the
    Atmosphere, The Austral. Phys. 19, 189-192.
Polikarpov, G. G., 1966: Radioecology of Aquatic
    Organisms, translated by Scripta Technica,
    Ltd., Reinhold Book Div., New York.
Turco, R. P., O. B. Toon, T. P. Ackerman, J. B.
    Pollack, C. Sagan, 1983: Nuclear winter:
    global consequences on multiple nuclear
    explosions, Science, 222, 1283-1292.
U. S. Congress, 1982: The Consequences of
    Nuclear War on the Global Environment,
    Hearing before Committee on Science and
    Technology, U.S. House of Representatives,
    Government Printing Office.
Wieseltier, L., 1983: Nuclear War, Nuclear
    Peace, A New Republic Book/Holt, Rinehart
    and Winston, New York.
Woodwell, G. M. and R. H. Whittaker, 1968:
    Efects of chronic gamma irradiation on plant
    communities, Q. Rev. of Biology, 43, 42-55.
World Health Organization, (Bergström, S. et
    al.), 1983: Effects of a Nuclear War on
    Health and Health Services, report of the
    International Committee of Experts in
    Medical Sciences and Public Health, WHO
    Publication A36.12, Geneva.

# 2. The Short-Term Consequences of Nuclear War for Civilians

## Abstract

Much of the debate over nuclear weapons policy continues to revolve around discussions of the usefulness of nuclear attacks on military targets. Much less attention, however, is devoted to either the number or the importance of the civilian casualties that such attacks would cause.

The short-term civilian casualties that would result from the use of nuclear weapons at three different levels of "limited nuclear war" are considered. These levels range from the employment of neutron bombs during an otherwise "conventional" battle in the Germanies to a nuclear attack against the strategic forces of the U.S. In addition, the consequences of all-out attacks by the superpowers on each other's cities are briefly discussed. It is found that nuclear planners and strategists have almost always grossly underestimated the human costs of the use of nuclear weapons.

## Introduction

It is widely believed that, if one of the superpowers resorted to the use of nuclear weapons, the subsequent exchanges might well escalate to all-out nuclear war. It is also widely believed that neither superpower can hope, by attacking the nuclear forces of the other, to eliminate the possibility of its own destruction. These beliefs are major deterrents to the use of nuclear weapons.

The U.S. defense posture vis à vis the Soviet Union in Europe, the Persian Gulf, and elsewhere is, however, based on another premise: that the U.S. is willing, if necessary, to initiate the use of nuclear weapons to stop the Soviet Union from crossing certain imaginary lines that have been drawn around areas the U.S. considers to be of "vital interest."

In order for this threat of first nuclear use to be credible to the Soviets, however, it is first necessary to convince ourselves that the benefits would outweigh the costs. This may explain why there is little discussion in the official literature of the considerations that might discourage the use of nuclear weapons.

The principal subject of this paper is one of these neglected areas: the unintended immediate casualties among civilians that would result from the use of nuclear weapons on military targets. The longer-term effects are discussed in subsequent chapters. In these estimates we take account of the likely effects of short-term radiation fallout of the type described by Upton in chapter 5 but we do not consider the long-term fallout effects on people or on ecosystems as outlined in chapters 5 and 6. The casualty figures discussed in this chapter are therefore on the very low side, and provide a minimum to which should be added estimates of the broader environmental effects. We discuss here the civilian fatalities that would result from the use of nuclear weapons for several cases that we and others have analyzed in some depth:

- Battlefield use in the Germanies (East and West) against conventional forces such as tanks;
- Use on the "theater" level--also in the Germanies--against medium- and intermediate-range nuclear weapon systems and nuclear warhead storage depots;
- Use against missile silos, bomber bases, and nuclear naval support facilities in the U.S.; and
- Use against the cities of the superpowers.

## Battlefield Use of Nuclear Weapons

Any major conflict on the conventional level between the superpowers would bring with it the danger that the losing side would resort to battlefield nuclear weapons. In Europe, this threat of "escalation" is implicit in the deployment of thousands of short-range nuclear warheads and delivery systems by the NATO and WTO (Warsaw Treaty Organization) forces.

According to the U.S. Army Field Manual (U.S. Army, 1982), U.S. battlefield nuclear systems are designed for use against

- Enemy nuclear delivery systems.
- Key command and control elements.
- Support forces in the rear of committed elements.
- Follow-on or deep-echeloned forces; and
- Reserves.

Battlefield nuclear systems range from atomic demolition mines, with explosive yields on the order of ten tons (0.01 kiloton) TNT equivalent, to bombs carried by tactical fighter-bombers, with yields of over one million tons (one megaton) TNT equivalent. Between these extremes in both yield and range are nuclear artillery shells and short-range surface-to-surface ballistic missiles (Cochran et al., 1983).

The Field Manual also describes how NATO use of these weapons would be authorized in "packages:"

A package is a group of nuclear weapons of specific yields for use in a specific area and within a limited time to support a specific tactical goal. Each package must contain nuclear weapons sufficient to alter the tactical situation decisively and to accomplish the mission.

The 1976 edition of the Field Manual gives as an example a package consisting of 2 atomic demolition mines (ADM), 30 rounds of nuclear artillery, 10 surface-to-surface missiles, and 5 air-delivered bombs (see Fig. 2-1).

Efforts would, of course, be made in planning and targeting such a set of nuclear warheads to minimize "collateral damage" to populated areas. This would be hard to do. The most-discussed hypothetical nuclear battlefield in the world in Europe and the most heavily nuclearized region in Europe is the two Germanies. The average popu-

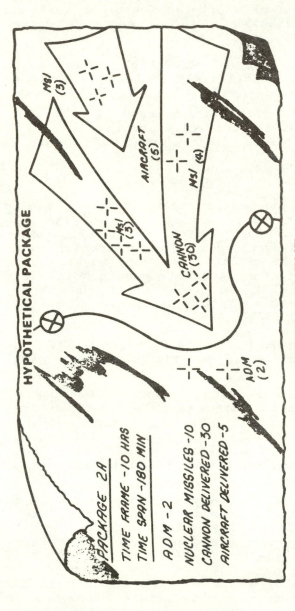

**EMPLOYMENT**

Fig. 2-1. A hypothetical "package" of battlefield nuclear weapons being delivered in front of and on the spearhead and follow-up formations of an attacking ground force. It includes 2 atomic demolition mines (ADM), 30 nuclear projectiles fired by artillery ("cannon"), 10 warheads delivered by short-range battlefield missiles ("Msl"), and 5 nuclear bombs delivered by aircraft (U.S. Army, 1976).

**EFFECTS OF A ONE KILOTON NEUTRON WARHEAD**

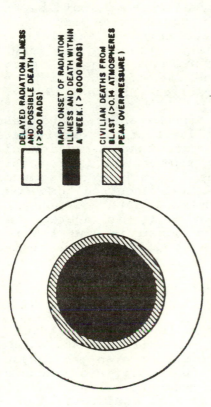

DELAYED RADIATION ILLNESS
AND POSSIBLE DEATH
(> 200 RADS)

RAPID ONSET OF RADIATION
ILLNESS AND DEATH WITHIN
A WEEK (> 8000 RADS)

CIVILIAN DEATHS FROM
BLAST (>0.14 ATMOSPHERES
PEAK OVERPRESSURE)

**450 METER ALTITUDE BURST**

0    0.5    1    2    3km.

0    1    2 mi.

Fig. 2-2. Lethal Areas Around Ground Zero for a Neutron Bomb Exploded at an Altitude of 450 Meters. The innermost circle shows the area of desired military effect: rapid onset of debilitating radiation illness. The slightly larger circle shows the area of serious blast damage to civilian structures. And the largest circle shows the area in which unshielded persons would receive large enough radiation doses to cause death from radiation illness within two months (von Hippel, 1983).

lation density of this area is 200 persons per square kilometer, with one populated place per four square kilometers (Arkin et al., 1982). Additional targeting difficulties would flow from the fact that roads naturally pass through these cities, towns, and villages and therefore so would many of the military units that would be the targets of battlefield nuclear weapons. In many cases, the roads between towns would be crowded with refugees. Finally, attacking military forces might use urban and refugee "hugging" tactics so as to discourage the use of battlefield nuclear weapons against themselves (Bracken, 1979).

Under these circumstances, and assuming short-term fallout effects of the magnitude specified in chapter 5, more than a million civilian deaths could result from the use of battlefield nuclear weapons at a militarily significant level. Even a one-kiloton neutron bomb would expose an area of about 5 square kilometers, populated in the Germanies by an average of 1000 people, to radiation doses in the lethal range (see Fig. 2-2), and it would require more than one thousand such explosions to immobilize a significant fraction of the 20,000 tanks that might be involved in a full-scale battle between NATO and WTO forces in the Germanies (Arkin et al., 1982).

Unfortunately, it is not clear that nuclear planners understand the horrendous carnage that would result from the use of even the lowest-yield nuclear warheads on the battlefield. According to Paul Bracken (1979), much of U.S. nuclear planning is based on the results of computerized war games that predict thousands, not millions, of civilian fatalities from the use of nuclear weapons on the battlefield. He reports that these very low fatality numbers are obtained because the computers are programmed to assume that there are no refugees on the roads and to

> treat Soviet forces as automata who cross into West Germany and advance directly into [unpopulated] NATO nuclear killing zones. Here they are detected and destroyed by the lowest yield nuclear weapon capable of doing the job. Command and control difficulties, confusion, false targeting and other problems are simply assumed away . . . What actually prevents either side from getting too close

to the 4000 towns and cities in Germany is a collection of Fortran statements (Bracken, 1979).

## Preemptive Use of Nuclear Weapons in Europe

Clearly, the consequences for civilian populations of even the use of relatively low-yield nuclear weapons on the battlefield could be catastrophic. And, it is quite possible that, in a crisis so severe that it resulted in the crossing of the nuclear threshold, the use of nuclear weapons would spread from the front lines. Indeed, both superpowers have deployed in Europe medium- and intermediate-range (up to about 5000 km for the Soviet SS-20 missile) nuclear weapon systems to back up their short-range battlefield nuclear systems. There are approximately 2000 warheads on land- and submarine-based missiles with ranges greater than 150 km in and around Europe plus nuclear bombs for an estimated 2500 nuclear-capable fighter-bombers and medium-range bombers. These warheads range in yield from about one kiloton to more than one megaton (Arkin et al., 1982).

These "theater" nuclear weapon systems are intended to destroy a whole range of targets:

IRBM/MRBM [Intermediate and Medium Range Ballistic Missile] sites; naval bases; nuclear and chemical storage sites; airbases; command, control, and communication centers; headquarters complexes; surface-to-air missile sites; munitions and petroleum storage areas and transfer facilities; ground forces installations; choke points; troop concentrations; and bridges (U.S. House Comm. on For. Affairs and Sen. For. Rel. Comm., 1980).

This list corresponds to over one thousand potential targets in the Germanies alone (Arkin et al., 1982).

There are, to our knowledge, no official estimates of the civilian casualties that might result from the use of a significant fraction of these theater nuclear weapons on their intended targets. In order to gauge the possible consequences, therefore, an independent calculation was recently undertaken. The scenario examined involved an attack limited to the nuclear targets in the above list located in the Germanies (Arkin et

25

al., 1982). This target set comprised a total of 171 surface-to-surface missile sites, military air bases and nuclear weapons storage depots (see Fig. 2-3). It would be natural to give these targets the highest priority since they pose the greatest destructive threat to the opposing forces in this region. It was assumed that each would be targeted by one or two 200-kiloton warheads.

The resulting civilian casualties in the two Germanies were estimated to range from 1.5-11 million deaths (7-25 million total casualties). The low figures were obtained by assuming that one 200-kiloton warhead exploded at an altitude of 2 kilometers over each target--too high to cause local fallout. The high figures were obtained by assuming attacks with two warheads--one air-burst and one ground-burst--on each target. This latter type of attack was assumed for "time urgent" targets such as nuclear air bases by NATO planners in a recent war-game (Campbell, 1981).

Thus, even the very limited use of theater nuclear weapons assumed in this scenario against purely military targets would leave a large fraction of the 76 million people living in the two Germanies dead and injured. These casualty estimates do not include the deaths that would result from the radioactive fallout carried by the wind into neighboring countries. (Fig. 2-4 shows the projected fallout pattern from the groundbursts using "typical June winds.") Nor do they include longer-term deaths, such as those from radiation-induced cancers, exposure, starvation, and epidemics.

Once again, the attacks envisioned in this scenario are very restrained--both in terms of the types of targets attacked and the small fraction of the available nuclear arsenal used. This restraint does not seem very plausible. All of the land-based nuclear delivery systems in Europe are vulnerable to nuclear attack, and the initiation of nuclear warfare would result in enormous pressures being put on nuclear decision-makers to "use them or lose them."

## Preemptive Strikes at the Intercontinental Level

The leaders of both superpowers have stated that the use of theater nuclear weapons in a regional war would probably result in further esca-

26

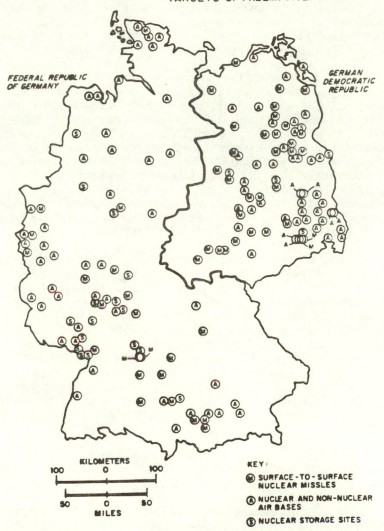

Fig. 2-3. Nuclear Targets in the Germanies. The area of each circle is 180 square kilometers —approximately equal to the area of destruction below a 200 kiloton warhead exploded at an altitude of 2 kilometers (Arkin et al., 1982).

lation to the use of long-range "strategic" nuclear weapons against targets located in the U.S. and the Soviet Union. Indeed, a principal argument for the deployment of U.S. cruise and Pershing II missiles in Western Europe is that, since these weapons can reach deep into the Soviet Union, they will make it even more difficult to limit nuclear war to Central Europe.

At the intercontinental level, the highest priority targets for each side would once again be the nuclear forces of the other side. In fact, much of the history of the nuclear arms race is that of efforts by each side to make the other side's nuclear weapon-systems more vulnerable to attack while trying to decrease the vulnerability of its own. The MX missile, for example, was originally intended both to increase the U.S. threat to Soviet ICBMs and to be less vulnerable than existing U.S. Minuteman missiles to attack by those same Soviet ICBMs.

As we have seen, almost no official information has been made available to the public about the civilian fatalites that could result from the use of nuclear weapons on the battlefield or theater levels. More information has been made available in the case of intercontinental attacks against strategic nuclear forces, however, because of a controversy triggered in 1974 when the Secretary of Defense, James Schlesinger, argued that the U.S. should be better prepared to respond "to a limited attack on military targets that caused relatively few civilian casualties" (Schlesinger, 1974).

The idea that a nuclear attack on the U.S. would not inevitably kill vast numbers of people was a novel one. Schlesinger was therefore questioned in March, 1974, at a Senate Foreign Relations subcommittee hearing, as to what he meant by "relatively few civilian casualties." He replied, "I am talking here about casualties of 15,000, 20,000, 25,000 . . ." (U.S. Sen. For. Rel. Comm., 1974a). The Senators were not satisfied with this answer, however. Schlesinger was asked to return and give them a briefing "on the consequences of the wide ranges of possible antimilitary attacks against the U.S." (U.S. Sen. For. Rel. Comm., 1974b).

28

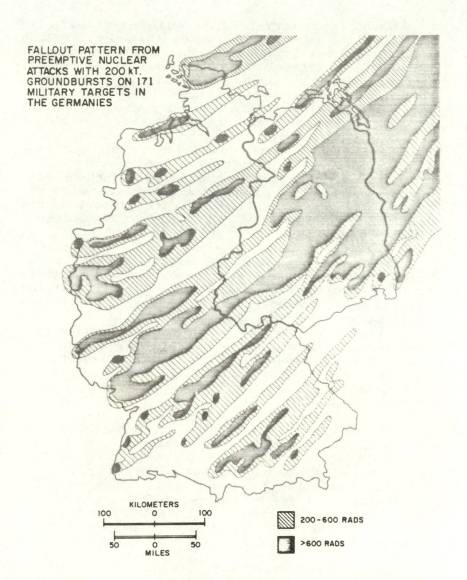

FALLOUT PATTERN FROM
PREEMPTIVE NUCLEAR
ATTACKS WITH 200 kT.
GROUNDBURSTS ON 171
MILITARY TARGETS IN
THE GERMANIES

KILOMETERS
100      0      100

50      0      50
MILES

▨ 200-600 RADS

▥ >600 RADS

Fig. 2-4.  Fallout from 200-kiloton ground-bursts on
the targets shown in Fig. 2-3, given "typical
June winds".   The black areas are those where
the radiation levels would be lethal to unsheltered persons.   The shaded areas are those in
which the radiation levels would be high enough
to cause severe radiation illness (Arkin et al.,
1982).

29

When Secretary Schlesinger returned in September, he reported estimates that the civilian casualties resulting from an all-out Soviet "counterforce attacks" against U.S. ICBM silos, strategic bomber bases, and nuclear navy bases might total about one million (U.S. Sen. For. Rel. Comm., 1974b). The Senators were still not satisfied, however, and asked the Congressional Office of Technology Assessment (OTA) to set up an outside review of the assumptions that had been made in the DOD calculations. Ultimately, as a result of the OTA group's criticisms, the DOD analysts revised many of their assumptions with the result that their fatality estimates rose into the range of 3-16 million (U.S. Sen. For. Rel. Comm., 1975).

Below, we consider separately the DOD's fatality estimates for attacks against the three sets of nuclear targets which were considered: ICBM silos, strategic bomber bases, and nuclear naval bases. We will discuss both the extent to which they were revised as a result of the expert panel's criticisms and the extent to which we find even the revised estimates to be an inadequate representation of the potential consequences of these nuclear attacks.

## Attacks on ICBM Fields

The bulk of the warheads involved in an attack against U.S. strategic nuclear forces would be thrown against the ICBM force--currently 1000 Minuteman missiles and approximately 50 Titan II missiles--and their associated launch-control facilities. These missiles and launch-control facilities are distributed across the Great Plains and Southwestern U.S. in six major and three minor missile "fields" (see Fig. 2-5).

Since these missile fields are generally located in relatively sparsely populated areas, the blast and heat of Soviet warheads exploding over them would cause relatively few civilian casualties. The missile silos and launch control centers are so hardened, however, that in order to subject one to sufficient overpressure to destroy it, a nuclear warhead would have to be exploded at such a low altitude that the fireball would touch the ground. As a result, such dirt and debris would be sucked up into the fireball, be contaminated with fission products, and subsequently fall

30

## FALLOUT FROM AN ATTACK ON U.S. MISSILE SILOS

**FATALITIES**

- ⬛️ GREATER THAN 50%, INDOORS ABOVE GROUND
- ▢ GREATER THAN 50%, OUTDOORS

- ■ MINUTEMAN FIELDS
- ☐ TITAN FIELDS

**ASSUMPTIONS**

- ○ 2 – ONE MEGATON WARHEADS ON EACH SILO
- ● 50 % FISSION YIELD
- ● SURFACE BURSTS
- ● TYPICAL MARCH WINDS

Fig. 2-5. Predicted fallout pattern, given "typical March winds" from 2 one-megaton warheads sur- face-burst on each U. S. ICBM silo. Within the shaded areas the cumulative biological doses of radiation would rise above the 450 rad average lethal level—even for people who stayed shel- tered indoors, where the radiation level is assumed to be one third of that outdoors (U. S. Sen. For. Rel. Comm., 1975).

to earth as radioactive fallout downwind from the target. Most of the fatalities associated with attacks on U.S. ICBM silos were found to be due to radiation doses from this fallout.

When Schlesinger first returned to brief the Senate Foreign Relations subcommittee on counter-force attacks, he described an attack on U.S. ICBM's in which a single one megaton warhead was exploded at its "optimum height of burst" over each silo and the resulting fallout was carried downwind by "typical August winds." The DOD analysts also assumed that, by the time the fallout had reached the cities downwind a few hours later, the residents would have all found places in the best available below-ground fallout shelters and that they would have the discipline and supplies to stay there for about two weeks. With these assumptions, the DOD's computers found that an attack on U.S. ICBM's would result in about 800,000 fatalities (U.S. Sen. For. Rel. Comm., 1974b).

The review committee found some of these assumptions to be optimistic, however, and therefore suggested that the DOD recalculate its numbers with different, more realistic assumptions. Some of the more important suggestions were the following (U.S. Sen. For. Rel. Comm., 1975):

● Since a single air-burst would not maximize the probability of destroying a missile silo, a surface-burst should be assumed as well. (A surface-burst would, however, increase the intensity of the radioactive fallout severalfold.);
● The sensitivity of the results to different wind conditions should be investigated. (As a result, the DOD analysts found that the greatest casualties would result with "typical March [not August] winds".); and
● Less optimistic assumptions should be made about the use of fallout shelters. (The DOD therefore made calculations assuming that about 45 percent of the population did not stay in below-ground shelters.)

As a result of these changes, the DOD's casualty estimates increased by an order of magnitude. It was now estimated that the U.S. would suffer as many as 5 million fatalities from an attack with two 550 kiloton warheads exploded over each ICBM silo (one at the surface and one at "optimum height-of-burst") and as many as 18 million deaths if the warhead yields were increased to 3 megatons (U.S. Sen. For. Rel. Comm., 1975).

The lower (550 kiloton) yield warheads assumed are near the low end of the range (0.5 to 1.0 megatons) ordinarily assumed for the yields of the multiple warheads on Soviet SS-17, SS-18, and SS-19 missiles (Tinajero, 1981). The higher (3 megaton) yield warheads fall outside of this range, but there is another scenario that would result in approximately this megatonnage being deposited on the ICBM fields. This would involve a one megaton surface-burst on each missile silo and a 20 megaton surface-burst on the hardened launch control facility that is associated with each "flight" of ten Minuteman silos. It is believed that in the 1960s, U.S. ICBM launch-control facilities were each targeted with one or two of the single very heavy (estimated 10-20 megaton yield) warheads carried by SS-9 missiles (Berman and Baker, 1982). The SS-18 missile, which has replaced the SS-9, has also been flight-tested with a single heavy warhead, although most are believed to carry 8-10 lighter warheads (Tinajero, 1981).

Fig. 2-5 shows that, given "typical March winds," the overlapping fallout patterns from individual missile silos would result in lethal levels of fallout covering hundreds of thousands of square kilometers and extending to distances of greater than one thousand kilometers downwind from the Minuteman fields. Cumulative radiation doses inside intact houses in the shaded areas would exceed 450 rads. The radiation dose-lethality curve shown in Fig. 2-6 indicates that a 450 rad dose would result in approximately a 50 percent fatality rate in the exposed population.

### Attacks on Nuclear Bomber Bases

A Soviet counterforce attack would also be expected to target the 19 U.S. Strategic Air Command (SAC) bases that are the permanent bases for U.S. intercontinental nuclear bombers and the additional SAC bases that host the tanker aircraft that would refuel these bombers during their missions or would act as dispersal bases during a crisis (Berman and Baker, 1982). Fig. 2-7 shows the locations of the 46 SAC bases to which these missions were assigned in 1974 (U.S. Sen. For.

33

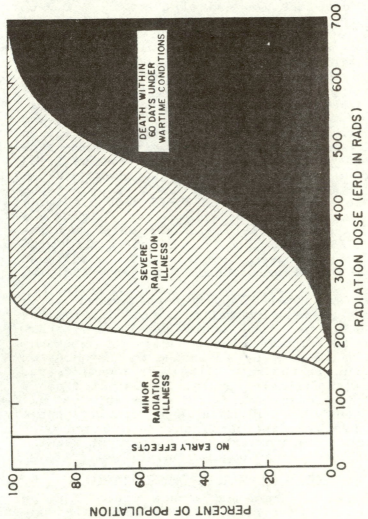

Fig. 2-6. The approximate probability of radiation illness and death as a function of accumulated whole-body dose (Arkin et al., 1982).

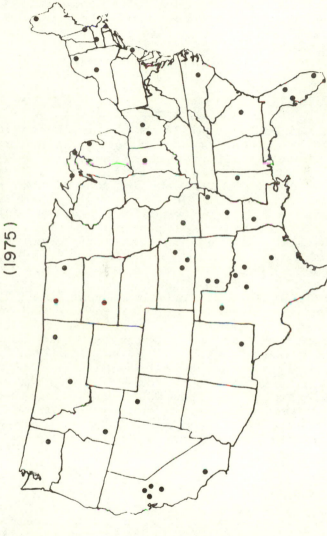

US STRATEGIC AIR COMMAND
OPERATIONAL BOMBER AND TANKER AIR BASES
(1975)

Fig. 2-7. The locations of U. S. nuclear bomber, tanker, and dispersal bases as of 1975 (U. S. Sen. For. Rel. Comm., 1975).

Rel. Comm., 1975; see, also, Air Force Magazine, 1982). Some of these SAC bases are located quite close to urban areas. The blast and heat from nuclear explosions over these air bases would therefore result in many more casualties than would be the case for the relatively isolated missile silos. Below, we attempt to reproduce the DOD estimates of civilian fatalities from nuclear attacks on these air bases and then explore some of the uncertainties in the assumptions used in making these estimates.

## The DOD Fatality Estimates

In his September 1974 testimony, Secretary of Defense Schlesinger presented estimates indicating that 300,000 fatalities would result if a single one megaton warhead were exploded at an "optimum height-of-burst" above each of the 46 SAC bases shown in Fig. 2-7. The only other information given was that "August winds" and "maximum utilization of existing civil defense facilities" had been assumed and that "the fatality level is 450 REM's or 7 psi, etc." (U.S. Sen. For. Rel. Comm., 1974b).

Although Schlesinger's statement about "fatality levels" is rather cryptic, a 450 REM whole-body radiation dose is the level at which approximately one half of the population would contract fatal radiation sickness. (See Fig. 2-6. Rems may be taken equivalent to rads in this case.) It is only natural to infer from Schlesinger's statement, therefore, that the DOD used a similar curve for the blast effects of nuclear explosions with the 50 percent fatality level being reached at approximately 7 pounds per square inch (psi)[1] peak overpressure.

This is, in fact, a characterisitic of the fatality probability versus-overpressure curve which can be derived from the curve shown in Fig. 2-8a (Oughterson and Warren, 1956) giving the probability of death as a function of distance from ground zero at Hiroshima. (The low "tail" on the fatality curve beyond 3 km in Fig. 2-8a presumably reflects an imperfection in the survey

---

[1]Because of its nearly universal usage in the nuclear-weapons-effects literature, we have not converted pounds per square inch into metric units in the text. One psi = 0.0689 Bars.

used and has been suppressed in our parameterization of the curve.) Fig. 2-8b shows this fatality curve replotted as a function of peak
ground-level overpressure. It has been assumed
that the yield of the Hiroshima bomb was 15 kilotons (Loewe and Mendelsohn, 1982) and that its
height-of-burst was 500 meters (Glasstone and
Dolan, 1977). Note that the 50 percent fatality
level is indeed reached at approximately 7 psi.
It is virtually certain that the DOD used a curve
such as that in Fig. 2-8b to make its estimates of
the casualties due to the blast and heat effects
of nuclear explosions.

Fig. 2-9 shows the total cumulative population as a function of distance from the 46 SAC
bases shown in Fig. 2-7 (FEMA, 1983). It will be
seen that approximately six million people live
within 10 miles of these bases. Given the relationship in Fig. 8b between the probability of
death and peak blast overpressure, and given
curves for this overpressure as a function of
height-of-burst and distance from ground zero for
a one megaton explosion (Glasstone and Dolan,
1977), one can calculate the total number of fatalities around the 46 SAC airbases as a function
of height-of-burst. The results are shown in
Fig. 2-10. It will be seen that the DOD's 300,000
fatalities correspond to a height-of-burst of
about 5 kilometers.

This height-of-burst is consistent with the
DOD's subsequent statement that the assumed attacks on the SAC bases would result in the "destruction of any aircraft flying within 2 to 3 nm
[nautical miles] of any of the 46 targets SAC
bases" (U.S. Sen. For. Rel. Comm., 1975). The
peak overpressure from a one-megaton airburst at
an altitude of 5 kilometers would be approximately
3 psi at a distance of about 3 nautical miles (5.5
km) from ground zero (Glasstone and Dolan, 1977).
This is approximately the peak overpressure at
which Quanbeck and Wood (1976) state that "large
aircraft of transport types are likely to receive
. . . severe damage."

A 5 kilometer height-of-burst is, however,
approximately 1.5 times the height-of-burst that
would maximize the area on the ground subjected to
a peak overpressure of 3 psi by a one megaton explosion (Glasstone and Dolan, 1977). It therefore

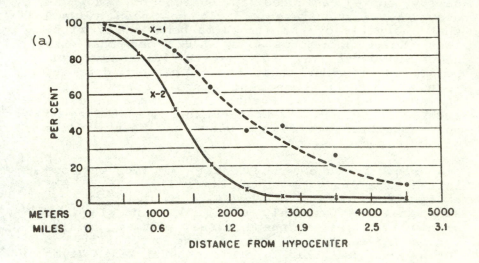

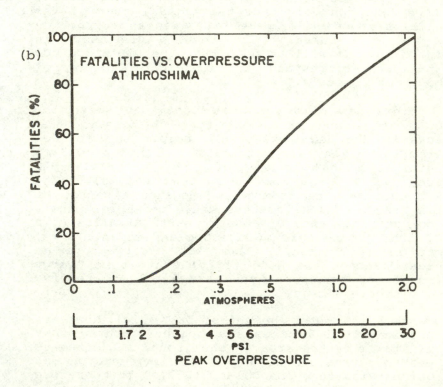

38

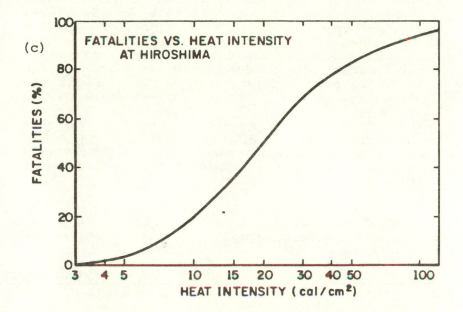

Fig. 2-8. Fatalities at Hiroshima as a function of:
a) distance from ground zero, b) peak overpressure, and c) time-integrated thermal radiation intensity. The original data are shown in
Fig. 2-8a (Oughterson and Warren, 1956) where
the small "x" symbols indicate the total mortality rate at different distances from ground
zero, "x-1" the mortality rate due to burns
among people in the open directly exposed to
the fireball, and "x-2" the mortality rate from
ionizing radiation among people shielded from
the termal radiation. The dashed curve in
Fig. 2-8a indicates the total incidence of mortality plus severe injury.

appears that, as with their initial assumptions about the likely characteristics of a Soviet attack on U.S. ICBM silos, the DOD analysts chose a height-of-burst for the attack on the SAC bases that would limit civilian fatalities in exchange for some lessening of the desired military effect. As Fig. 2-10 shows, if the height-of-burst had been lowered to approximately 3 kilometers, where the area subjected to overpressure greater than 3 psi (and therefore the military effectiveness of the attack) would be maximized, the estimated number of deaths would have more than tripled to about one million. This is not the whole story, however. As will be shown below, it was inappropriate for the DOD to assume that the level of fatalities resulting from one megaton airbursts high over U.S. bomber bases would be the same function of overpressure as the fatalities that resulted from a 15 kiloton airburst over Hiroshima.

### Heat Effects

In Hiroshima, the heat from the fireball was intense enough to give most unsheltered people fatal skin burns out to distances of 2 kilometers (Oughterson and Warren, 1956). The amount of heat energy deposited on an exposed surface facing the explosion at this distance was about 8 cal/cm$^2$ and the peak blast overpressure was 3.5 psi.

It would take a somewhat greater intensity from a one megaton airburst (about 11 cal/cm$^2$) to be as damaging because of the longer duration of the thermal pulse (Glasstone and Dolan, 1977). If the one megaton explosion occurred at an altitude of 5 kilometers on a clear day, the thermal radiation intensity would exceed this level out to approximately 13 km from ground zero. At this distance, however, the corresponding peak overpressure would be only about 1.5 psi--too low according to the overpressure model shown in Fig. 8b to cause a significant percentage of deaths. It appears, therefore, that in this case the heat effects of the nuclear explosion must be explicitly taken into account.

We have therefore fitted the Hiroshima fatality data with a family of simple models that give variable relative weights to the importance of blast and heat. (These models still ignore the

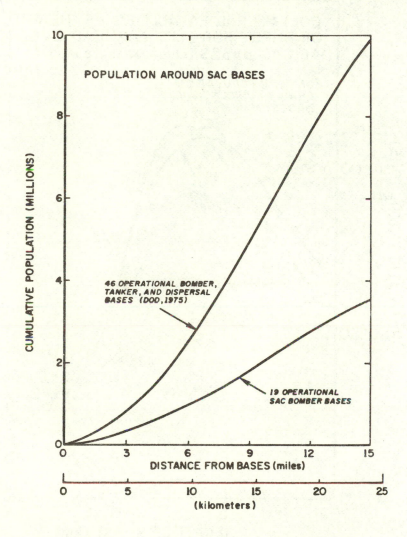

Fig. 2-9.    Summed cumulative populations as  a
     function of  distance  from the centers of
     19 operational Strategic Air Command (SAC)
     bases and all 46 SAC  bomber-related  (in-
     cluding tanker and dispersal) bases.

41

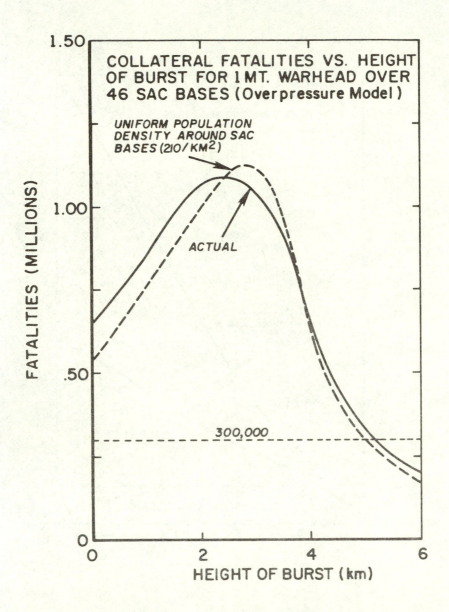

Fig. 2-10. Fatalaties calculated using the curve in Fig. 2-8b—given a one megaton explosion over each of the 46 SAC bases—as a function of the height-of-burst.

fact that, at distances closer than 1 km to ground zero at Hiroshima, people not shielded by thick walls were exposed to lethal doses of gamma radiation from the explosion. Most of these people would, however, have been killed by blast or burn effects in any case. For nuclear explosions of higher yields, the lethal range of the "prompt" nuclear radiation emitted by the explosion would be buried still deeper within the area of lethal blast and heat effects.)

At one extreme of our family of fatality models is the "DOD model," corresponding to the curve in Fig. 8b in which all deaths are assumed to be due to overpressure (blast) effects. For our calculations, we have parameterized this Probability of Death due to overPressure as

$$P_{DP} = \exp[-.69^*(7.4/p)^{1.4}],$$

where p is the peak overpressure in psi.

At the other extreme, we assume that all the deaths at Hiroshima were due to heat. We then have a parameterization of the curve in Fig. 8c as the Probability of Death due to Heat

$$P_{DH} = 1 - \exp[-.69^*(19^*f/H)^{1.3}],$$

where H is the heat intensity in cal/cm$^2$. The factor f is equal to unity for a nuclear explosion with the yield of the Hiroshima bomb but must be increased for greater yields to take into account the decrease in burn-effectiveness of the thermal radiation of the associated longer thermal pulse (Glasstone and Dolan, 1977).

Fig. 2-11 shows the fatality levels predicted by the two extreme models for a one megaton warhead exploded at an altitude of 5 kilometers, as a function of distance from ground zero. It will be seen that the thermal effect model would predict a much higher number of fatalities in this case than the overpressure model used by the DOD--even though the parameters of both models are fixed to predict the same distribution of fatalities for the yield and height-of-burst of the Hiroshima weapon.

Between the extreme models, we have a spectrum of models obtained by taking their weighted

43

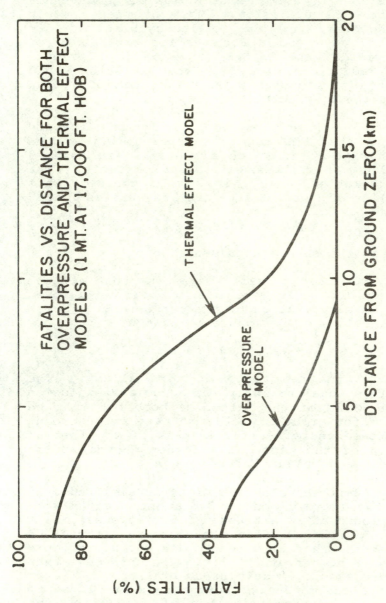

Fig. 2-11.    Comparison of the incidence of fatalities as a function of
distance from ground zero predicted by the overpressure and
heat models, given a one megaton warhead exploded at an altitude of 5 kilometers.

average:

$$P_D = (1 - w)^* P_{DB} + w^* P_{DH},$$

where w, the weighting factor, can take any value in the range between zero (DOD overpressure model) and unity (heat model). Given a one megaton airburst at a height of 5 kilometers above each of the 46 SAC bases, the corresponding fatality predictions range from the DOD's value of 300,000 to 1.85 million.

It is unclear what value of w might give the most "realistic" model. A value of w = .2, corresponding to a fatality prediction of about 600,000, might seem appropriate if one assumed that 20 percent of the population would be exposed to direct thermal radiation effects--either outdoors or near windows indoors. Higher values of w would be appropriate if the heat radiated by the fireball caused firestorms well beyond the areas of serious blast effects. In either case, it appears that the failure to explicitly consider heat effects in the DOD fatality model was a major omission.

## Pattern Attacks

In its critique of the original DOD casualty calculations, the Office of Technology Assessment's review group questioned the assumption that only one nuclear warhead would be used to attack each SAC bomber and tanker base. The panel suggested that it was more likely that the areas around each of the bases would be "pattern" attacked with a number of warheads in order to try to destroy in the air as many as possible of the aircraft that had taken off on warning of attack (U.S. Sen. For. Rel. Comm., 1975). The DOD responded by estimating the number of fatalities that would result from pattern attacks on the SAC bases but buried its results in the consequences of a more comprehensive attack. We have therefore made our own estimates, using the set of fatality models described above.

The only indication given by the DOD of the nature of the pattern attack that it had assumed is the statement that this attack would cause the "destruction on any A/C [aircraft] flying within 8 nm [nautical miles] of the 46 target SAC bases"

(U.S. Sen. For. Rel. Comm., 1975). This corresponds to an area of aircraft destruction 7-16 times as large as that which had been given for a single one megaton warhead attack (2-3 nm [3.7-5.6 km] radius).

We have therefore estimated the number of fatalities that would be caused by a pattern attack by assuming airbursts of 7-16 one megaton warheads distributed over a circle of 8 nm (15 km) in a radius around each of the 46 SAC bases. We have also simplified our calculation by assuming an average probability of death throughout this circle equal to the average probability of death throughout this circle equal to the average probability of death in a circle under a one megaton airburst with a radius of 3.7 km (16 warhead case) or 5.6 km (7 warhead case). Deaths that would occur outside the 15 km radius have been neglected. With these assumptions and an assumed height-of-burst of 5 km, we estimate 1.0-1.6 million fatalities with the DOD's overpressure model (w = 0) and 5.3-6.4 million fatalities with the pure thermal effects model (w = 1).

Ordinarily, in discussions of counterforce attacks against the U.S., it is assumed that the escape time of the bombers and tankers would be minimized by striking their bases with warheads launched from submarines located as close as possible to U.S. shores. In this context, the barrage attacks discussed above would appear implausible because the number of one megaton warheads required (322-736 for 46 SAC bases) is too large to be delivered by the small number of Soviet ballistic missile submarines ordinarily on patrol near the U.S.

Some of the newer Soviet submarine-launched missiles, however, appear to have multiple warheads of smaller yield. The SS-N-18, for example, is believed to be equipped with seven warheads, each with an estimated yield of 300 kilotons (Tinajero, 1981). At a height-of-burst of about 2 km, seven 200 kiloton warheads would be able to cover as large an area with peak-blast overpressures in excess of 3 psi as the seven one megaton warheads exploded at 5 kilometers in the hypothetical pattern attacks discussed above. In such a case, only one SS-N-18 missile would be required for a pattern attack against each of the

SAC bases for a total of 46 missiles in all—about as many as could be carried by three of the Soviet Union's 13-plus Delta III class submarines (Jane's Fighting Ships, 1982-83).

We have therefore estimated the consequences of a pattern attack with an SS-N-18 missile on each of the 46 SAC bases and find 1.6 million deaths using the overpressure model and 0.4 million using the heat model. (The prediction of the overpressure model is higher in this case because of the lower altitude of burst.) If one of the seven warheads were ground-burst for the purpose of cratering and radioactively contaminating the runway of each base, there would be an additional 40,000 fatalities from radioactive fallout (assuming "typical March winds").

Our conclusion from the above discussion is that the DOD's original estimates of the civilian fatalities from a nuclear attack on U.S. bomber and tanker bases were too low—but by a factor that is quite uncertain.

## Attacks on Nuclear Navy Bases

In peacetime, nearly half of U.S. ballistic missile submarines, (and therefore over 2000 U.S. strategic warheads) are located in four ports: Groton, Connecticut; Charleston, South Carolina; King's Bay, Georgia; and Bangor, Washington (Cochran et al., 1983). Other potential counterforce targets would be bases hosting attack submarines, aircraft carriers, and other ships carrying nuclear weapons that could be used to attack the Soviet Union or its navy. There are at least six such nuclear navy bases in the continental U.S. in addition to the four bases hosting ballistic missile submarines: Alameda, Long Beach, and San Diego, California; Mayport, Florida; Newport, Rhode Island; and Norfolk, Virginia (Cochran et al., 1983). (See Fig. 2-12.) Attacks on these bases would result in substantial numbers of fatalities in nearby urban areas.

In his 1974 briefing, Schlesinger presented an estimate of 250,000 fatalities resulting from an explosion of a one megaton warhead over four of the above ten naval bases (see Table 2-1). The assumed height-of-burst was not given.

47

## U.S. NUCLEAR NAVY BASES

**SSBN = BALLISTIC MISSLE SUBMARINE BASE**

Fig. 2-12.    Locations of the major bases in the continental U.S. out of which nuclear-armed naval ships operate.

Table 2-1

======================================================================

Estimated Civilian Fatalities from One Megaton
Ground-bursts on Ten Nuclear Navy Bases
(in thousands).

| Base | DOD[a] | This Work | | |
|---|---|---|---|---|
| | | Blast | Fallout | Total |
| **Ballistic Missile Submarine** | | | | |
| Bangor, WA | -- | 2 | 34-260 | 36-260 |
| Charleston, SC | 45 | 38 | 0- 15 | 38- 53 |
| Groton, CT | -- | 30 | 8-195 | 38-225 |
| King's Bay, GA | -- | 0 | 0 | 0 |
| **Other Nuclear Navy Bases** | | | | |
| Alameda, CA | -- | 55 | 22-485 | 77-540 |
| Long Beach, CA | 60 | 75 | 72-170 | 145-245 |
| Mayport, FL | -- | 8 | 0- 8 | 8- 16 |
| Newport, RI | -- | 8 | 4-110 | 12-115 |
| Norfolk, VA | 50 | 73 | 1-105 | 74-180 |
| San Diego, CA | 90 | 51 | 21-435 | 72-490 |
| | 245 | 340 | 160-1780 | 500-2120 |

Table 1, Notes

[a]U. S. Sen. For. Rel. Comm., 1974b.

49

We have estimated the number of civilian fa-
talities--from the blast and fallout--that would
result from an attack on each of the ten continental nuclear navy bases. A fallout program provided by the Federal Emergency Management Administration was adapted for this purpose (Schmidt,
Jr., 1975). A one megaton ground-burst was assumed as well as the most pessimistic distribution of
fallout protection factors used in the DOD's calculations (U.S. Sen. For. Rel. Comm., 1975).
Several "typical" winds--March, June, and
August--were used (Defense Communications Agency,
1981), resulting in a range of expected fatalities
due to fallout. Our results are given in Table
2-1.

Total fatalities in the areas surrounding the
ten naval bases were estimated to be 0.5 - 2.1
million. The contribution due to fallout varied
from less than a third to nearly all of the total,
depending upon the winds. "Typical March winds"
gave the lowest estimates while "typical August
winds" yielded the highest. In those cases where
a DOD estimate was made (Charleston, Long Beach,
Norfolk, and San Diego), the DOD figure lies near
the bottom or below the fatality range that we
calculated.

In a 1980 NATO war game designated "Operation
Squareleg" it was assumed that U.S. and British
missile submarine bases in Scotland would be attacked with ground-bursts of not one megaton, but
5-megaton warheads (Campbell, 1981). Our preliminary calculations show that the casualties resulting from a similar attack on the nuclear navy
bases in the U.S. would be several times higher
than in the one megaton case. The total number of
fatalities due to blast alone would rise from 340
to 990 thousand.

## Attacks on Nuclear Warning, Communications,
## Command, and Defense Facilities

In order to disrupt if not prevent a U.S.
nuclear response, the highest-priority targets of
a Soviet attack on the U.S. strategic nuclear system would be U.S. early warning systems, the command centers that would issue the orders for U.S.
nuclear weapons use, and the communication systems

that would transmit these orders.[2]  Presumably, an attempt would be made to destroy U.S. strategic defensive systems as well.  As a result of such considerations, Berman and Baker (1982) list, in addition to nuclear delivery systems and their local launch-control facilities, the following "nuclear threat targets" for Soviet intercontinental forces:

- 60 National Command Authority Centers;
- 5 airbases for airborne command posts;
- 60 transmitters for communicating with ballistic missile submarines;
- 132 radars;
- 28 fighter-interceptor sites; and
- 1 ABM test site.

Ball (1981) suggests that a number of ground stations linking the strategic "command-and-control" network to early warning, navigational, military communication, and meteorological satellites would also be targeted.

We have not yet estimated the casualties from an attack against the U.S. command-and-control system.  The numbers are likely to be large because there are hundreds of targets, and many are located near highly populated areas.  It is already evident from the above discussion, however, that U.S. deaths from a Soviet nuclear attack on U.S. strategic nuclear targets alone would probably number in the tens of millions--comparable to total Soviet losses in World War II--but incurred in a period of days or weeks instead of years.

## Attacks on Cities

In view of the horrendous, albeit unintended civilian casualties which would result from serious attacks against strategic weapons and their control systems, retaliation against the cities of the attacking nation would become quite credible.

## Attacks on Soviet Cities

In 1968, then Secretary of Defense Robert McNamara ordered the DOD to try to quantify the

--------

[2]These systems are sometimes denoted by the acronym C[3]I denoting Command, Control, Communications, and Intelligence.

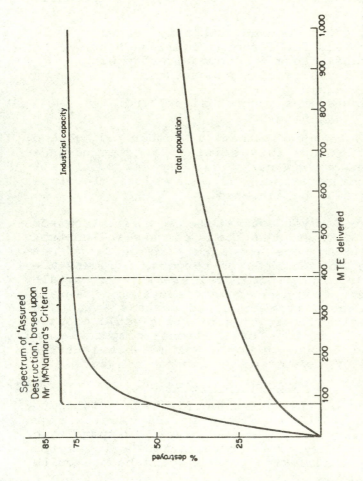

Fig. 2-13.  In 1968, then Secretary of Defense Robert McNamara published estimates of the percentages of the Soviet population and industrial
capacity that could be destroyed by the U. S. using 100, 200, 400,
800, 1200, and 1600 "equivalent megatons" of nuclear explosive
power (McNamara, 1968).  The above curves are interpolations of
these numbers made by Kemp (1974).

amount of destruction that the U.S. could inflict on the cities and industry of the Soviet Union as a function of the "equivalent megatonnage"[3] of nuclear warheads used. An interpolation of the results (McNamara, 1968) gives the curves shown in Fig. 2-13.

No explanation was given in McNamara's report about the assumptions used in calculating these results. In the case of population, however, a reasonable guess can be hazarded on the basis of a comparison of the "assured destruction" curve in Fig. 2-13, which shows cumulative Soviet fatalities as a function of equivalent megatons used, with the curve in Fig. 2-14, which shows the cumulative Soviet urban population as a function of urban land area. One finds from Fig. 2-15 that the 25 percent of the total Soviet population (50 percent of the urban population) that lives in the most densely populated urban areas of the Soviet Union lives on about 1000 square nautical miles (3500 square kilometers). According to Fig. 2-13, this many people could be killed by 270 equivalent megatons. Dividing the two numbers gives an "equivalent area of death" of about 13 square kilometers per equivalent megaton.

This equivalent area of death corresponds to the area of a circle approximately 2 km in radius. This is the area that could be subjected to an overpressure greater than 30 psi by an airbust or about 20 psi for a ground-burst (Glasstone and Dolan, 1977).

In Hiroshima, however, the equivalent area of death was approximately equal to the area subjected to an overpressure greater than 5 psi (von Hippel, 1983). If this criterion had been used in the calculations done for McNamara, the megatonnages shown along the horizontal axis of Fig. 2-14 would be lower by a factor of 5 for ground-bursts and up to a factor of 12 for air-bursts. Thus, the use of an equivalent area of death scaled from that at Hiroshima would, for example, lead to a

---

[3]The "equivalent megatonnage" of a nuclear weapon scales in the same way as the area that it can subject to more than a given peak blast overpressure: as the two-thirds power of the megatonnage.

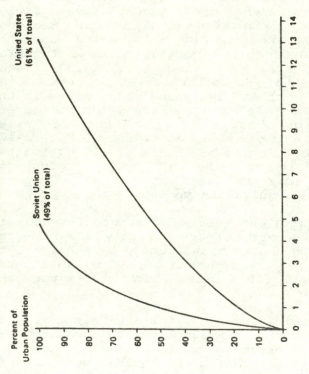

Fig. 2-14. Cumulative Soviet and U.S. urban populations as a function of land area, according to the U.S. Arms Control and Disarmament Agency (1978). One thousand square nautical miles (NM2) equals 3,420 square kilometers.

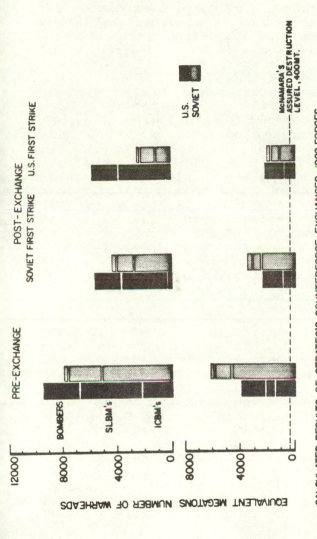

CALCULATED RESULTS OF STRATEGIC COUNTERFORCE EXCHANGES; 1982 FORCES
(BOTH SIDES ON GENERATED ALERT)

Fig. 2-15. Comparison of the U.S. and Soviet strategic arsenals as of 1982. The arsenals are measured here in terms of numbers of warheads (first row) and equivalent megatonnage (second row) as they existed (left hand side) and after hypothetical counterforce exchanges initiated by the USSR (middle) or the U.S. (right hand side). The surviving forces were estimated assuming that the exchanges occurred after a period of crisis and that both sides therefore had a greater than usual percentage of their ballistic missile submarines at sea and bombers on quick-reaction alert (Feiveson and von Hippel, 1983).

range of estimates of 20-40 equivalent megatons rather than the approximately 200 equivalent megatons that McNamara's DOD calculated would be required to kill 20-25 percent of the Soviet population. (The overlapping of circles of death with each other and with the edges of urban population areas would reduce the correction factors somewhat, but the addition of fallout effects and secondary effects such as illness and starvation among the survivors of the direct effects of the nuclear explosions would increase them.)

Fig. 2-15 shows that in 1983, even after absorbing a first strike, both the U.S. and USSR would have thousands of equivalent megatons in their surviving nuclear arsenals. A comparison with Fig. 2-14 shows that, even without taking into account the conservatism in the calculations done for McNamara, this explosive power is well into the "overkill" region for both the cities and industry of the USSR.

More recent studies have confirmed this conclusion with more detail. In one analysis, for example, the U.S. Arms Control and Disarmament Agency (U.S. ACDA, 1978) estimated that those U.S. strategic bombers and ballistic missile submarines surviving a Soviet first strike could subject 65 to 90 percent of "key Soviet production capacity" (primary metals, petroleum products, electric power generation, etc.) to peak overpressures in excess of 10 psi. The ACDA estimated that the same attack would also destory 60 to 80 percent of the remaining, non-targeted Soviet production capacity by "collateral damage".

The hypothetical U.S. attack in this case was directed against Soviet "strategic forces, other military targets, and industry"--not population. Nevertheless, it was estimated that, if the Soviet population remained in place, 80-95 million fatalities would result. It was also estimated that this number of fatalities could be reduced to 23-34 million if Soviet cities were evacuated. The ACDA pointed out, however, that its assumptions concerning the effectiveness of evacuation were extremely optimistic:

80 percent of the urban population evacuates the cities to range up to 150 km and the remaining 20 percent take protection in the

best available shelters. The evacuated
people are located with the rural population,
and both the evacuees and rural people go to
the best availale rural shelters and build
hasty shelters . . . This posture represents
an immense civil defense effort and no analysis was made to determine the feasibility of
implementing such a posture.

The report adds that, if "residual weapons [were
used] to directly target the evacuated population," the number of Soviet fatalities could be
increased back up to 54-65 million. None of these
fatality numbers include indirect deaths due to
exposure, starvation, lack of medical attention,
epidemics, etc.

## Attacks on U.S. Cities

The U.S. Federal Emergency Management Administration (FEMA, 1979) has designated certain areas
of the U.S. as "high risk areas" for civil nuclear
defense planning purposes. According to this report,

Potential target values were developed . . .
based on the following criteria listed in de-
scending priority order:
a. U.S. military installations
b. Military supporting industrial,
transportation and logistics facilities.
c. Other basic industries and
facilities which contribute significantly to
the maintenance of the U.S. economy.
d. Population concentrations of 50,000
or greater . . .
[Then, after taking into account] projections
of Soviet capabilities (circa 1980) . . . en-
velopes were plotted . . . to depict areas
subject to a 50 percent or greater probability of receiving blast overpressures of 2 psi
or more.

This hypothetical attack is also discussed
in a report published by Oak Ridge National Laboratory (Haaland et.,a 1976). (See Fig. 2-16.)
There, it is described as being associated with a
specific attack scenario involving a total of 1444
warheads with the following distribution of
yields: 20 megatons (241), 3 megaton (176), 2
megatons (184), and 1 megaton (843). This appears
to be the approximate distribution of yields which
the Soviet strategic arsenal would have if all

Hypothetical Nuclear Attack for Cross Relocation Planning.
Circles Show Areas Covered with 2 psi Or Greater over Pressure from Blast.
Number of Delivered Weapons: 1444.    Total Yield Delivered: 6559 Megatons.

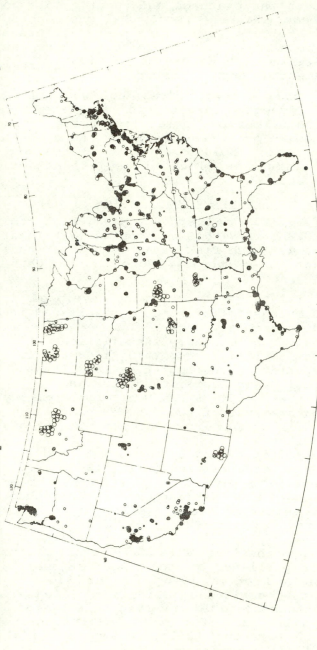

Fig. 2-16. CRP-2B Attack Pattern on the U.S.  The hypothetical Soviet attack used
by the Federal Emergency Management Administration for civil defense
planning purposes (Haaland et al., 1976).  The areas within the circles
would be subjected to peak overpressures in excess of  2  pounds  per
square inch.

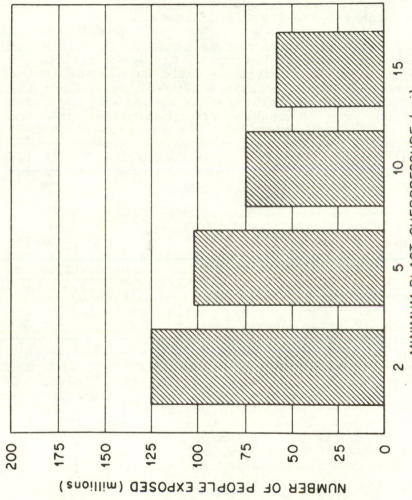

Fig. 2-17. Calculated exposure of the U.S. population to peak blast overpressures, given the attack shown in Fig. 2-16 and in the absence of urban evacuation (Haaland et al., 1976).

Soviet ballistic missiles carried single warheads. Since the scenario was devised, many of
these missiles have been replaced with missiles
carrying multiple independently-targetable warheads. In terms of both total and equivalent
megatonnage (6560 and 3300 respectively), however,
the attack is still physically possible (see Fig.
2-15) and does, according to FEMA (1979), cover
the highest priority U.S. targets.

Fig. 2-17 shows the estimate in the Oak Ridge
report of the distribution of overpressures to
which the U.S. population would be subject in the
absence of urban evacuation. Fig. 2-18 shows the
corresponding distribution of radiation doses from
fallout for an unsheltered population with and
without urban evacuation. It was assumed that 77
percent of the total megatonnage in the attack
would be ground-burst on military and industrial
targets and that the winds would be blowing due
east at 40 kilometers per hour.

The conversion between the "unit-time reference doses" shown in Fig. 2-18 and the peak e-
quivalent residual doses that parameterize the fatality curves in Fig. 2-6 involve factors on the
order of unity (Glasstone and Dolan, 1977). On
the basis of Fig. 2-17 (in combination with Fig.
2-8b) and/or Fig. 2-18 (in combination with Fig.
2-6) one can therefore conclude that, in the absence of urban evacuation and effective fallout
shelters for the evacuated population, about one-
half of the U.S. population would die in this
hypothetical attack. This is consistent with the
estimates by the Arms Control and Disarmament
Agency (U.S. ACDA, 1978) that a comprehensive
Soviet attack on the U.S. would result in 105-131
million U.S. fatalities in the absence of evacuation and 69-91 million with urban evacuation.
Once again, fatalities due to starvation, exposure, and disease were not estimated.

## Conclusions

Most discussions of "limited" nuclear war
focus solely on the political and military costs
and benefits. Typically, they take little or no
account of the possible consequences for civilian
populations of such uses of nuclear weapons. When
mentioned, these consequences are often dismissed
without any attempt at quantification as the unin-

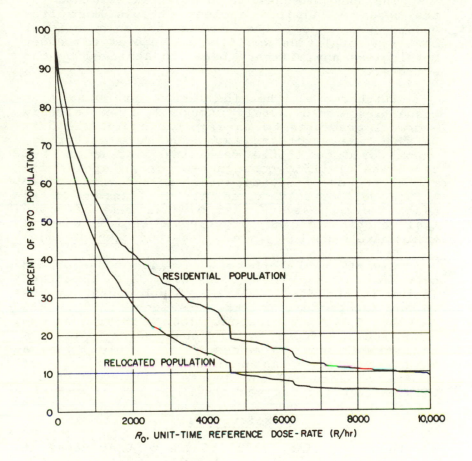

Fig. 2-18. Calculated exposure of the U. S.
population to radiation in the absence
of sheltering, given the attack shown
in Fig. 2-16 and easterly winds—with
and without evacuation of the cities
and towns (Haaland et al., 1976).

tended "collateral effects" of attacks aimed at purely military targets.

The above discussion shows, however, that for the types of limited nuclear attacks most frequently discussed, the number of unintentional civilian fatalities would be so huge as to render meaningless any military benefits achieved by the attacker.

Furthermore, the infliction of such high casualties would surely compound other already enormous pressures to move up the nuclear ladder. By the time strategic exchanges were occurring, there would be little remaining distinction between the civilian consequences of an attack directed at purely military targets and those of an attack deliberately aimed at civilians. It is also likely, however, that by this time all central control over the targeting of nuclear weapons would have been lost in any case [Bracken, 1983].

Clearly the short-term civilian consequences of the use of nuclear weapons will be an important factor in the determination of subsequent events in any future nuclear war. As such, they should be taken fully into account along with broader environmental effects by serious nuclear planners and strategists. The result is likely to be a more conservative assessment of the utility of nuclear weapons and the degree to which we should rely on them for our security.

## References

Air Force Magazine, 1982: Guide to USAF Bases at Home and Abroad, 65(7):188.

Arkin, W. M., F. von Hippel, and B. G. Levi, 1982: The effects of a "limited" nuclear war in East and West Germany, in Ambio XI(2-3): 163-173, Reprinted in Peterson, J. (ed.) The Aftermath: the Human and Ecological Consequences of Nuclear War, pp. 165-187, Pantheon, New York. See also addendum in Ambio XII(1):57.

Ball, D., 1981: Can nuclear war be controlled? Adelphi Paper #169, International Institute for Strategic Studies, London.

Berman, R. P., and J. C. Baker, 1982: Soviet Strategic Forces: Requirements and Responses, Brookings, Washington, D.C.

Bracken, P., 1979: On theater warfare, Hudson Institute, Report #HI-3036-P, Croton-on-Hudson, NY.

Bracken, P., 1983: The Command and Control of Nuclear Forces, Yale University Press, New Haven, CN.

Campbell, D., 1981: World war III: an exclusive preview, and Scotland's nuclear targets, in: Britain and the Bomb, pp. 65-70, New Statesman, London.

Cochran, T. B., W. M. Arkin, and M. M. Hoenig, 1983: Nuclear Weapons Data Book, Volume I: U.S. Nuclear Forces and Capabilities, Ballinger, Cambridge, MA.

Feiveson, H. A., and F. von Hippel, 1983: The freeze and the counterforce race. Physics Today 36(1):36.

FEMA, 1979: High risk areas for civil defense planning purposes, Federal Emergency Management Administration TR-82, Washington, D.C.

FEMA, 1983: The U.S. population distribution was provided on a computerized (two minute grid) data base provided us in 1983 by the Federal Emergency Management Administration, Washington, D.C.

Glasstone, S., and P. J. Dolan (eds.), 1977: The Effects of Nuclear Weapons, 3rd edition, U.S. Departments of Defense and Energy, Washington, D.C.

Haaland, C. M., C. V. Chester, and E. P. Wigner, 1976: Survival of the relocated population of the U.S. after a nuclear attack, Oak Ridge National Laboratory, ORNL-5041, Oak Ridge, TN.

Jane's Fighting Ships, 1982-83: (J. Moore, ed.), Jane's Publishing Co., London.

Kemp, G., 1974: Nuclear forces for medium powers part I: targets and weapons systems, Adelphi Paper #106, International Institute for Strategic Studies, London.

Loewe, W. E., and E. Mendelsohn, 1982: Neutron and gamma doses at Hiroshima and Nagasaki, in: Nuclear Science and Engineering 81:325.

McNamara, R., 1968: Statement before the Senate Armed Services Committee on the Fiscal Year 1969-73 Defense Program and 1969 Defense Budget, U.S. Department of Defense, Washington, D.C.

Oughterson, A. W., and S. Warren (eds.), 1956: Medical Effects of the Atomic Bomb in Japan, McGraw-Hill, New York.

Quanbeck, A. H., and A. L. Wood, 1976: Moderniz-
ing the Strategic Bomber Force: Why and How,
Brookings Institution, Washington, D.C.
Schlesinger, J. R., 1974: Annual Defense Depart-
ment Report, FY 1975, U.S. Department of
Defense, Washington, D.C.
Schmidt, Jr., L. A., 1975: Methodology of Fall-
out-Risk Assessment, Institute for Defense
Analyses, Paper P-1065, Arlington, VA.
Tinajero, A. A., 1981: U.S./USSR Strategic Offensive Weapons: Projected Inventories Based on
Carter Policies, Congressional Research Ser-
vice, Report 81-238 F, Washington, D.C.
U.S. ACDA, 1978: Analysis of civil defense in
nuclear war, U.S. Arms Control and Disarma-
ment Agency, Washington, D.C.
U.S. Army, 1976: Operations, Field Manual FM
100-5, Washington, D.C.
U.S. Army, 1982: Operations, Field Manual FM
100-5, Washington, D.C.
U.S. Defense Communications Agency, 1981: North-
ern hemisphere wind data for a "typical day"
in each month was provided by the Command and
Control Technical Center (unclassified tapes
EA 275 and EB 275).
U.S. House Comm. on For. Affairs and Sen. For.
Rel. Comm., 1980: Fiscal Year 1981 Arms Con-
trol Impact Statements, Joint Committee
Print, Washington, D.C.
U.S. Sen. For. Rel. Comm., 1974a: U.S. - USSR
Strategic Policies, Hearing before the Sub-
committee on Arms Control, International Law
and Organization, March 4, 1974, Washington,
D.C.
U.S. Sen For. Rel. Comm., 1974b: Briefing on
counterforce attacks, Hearing before the Sub-
committee on Arms Control, International Law,
and Organization, September 11, 1974,
Washington, D.C. (Reprinted in U.S. Sen.
For. Rel. Comm., 1975.)
U.S. Sen. For. Rel. Comm., 1975: Analyses of
Effects of Limited Nuclear Warfare, Committee
Print, Subcommittee on Arms Control, International Organization and Security Agreements
of the Senate Committee on Foreign Relations,
Washington, D.C.
von Hippel, F., 1983: The Effects of Nuclear War,
in Physics, Technology and the Arms Race (D.
W. Hafemeister and D. Schroeer, eds.), pp.
1-46, American Institute of Physics, New
York, NY.

# 3. Transport and Residence Times of Airborne Radioactivity

### Abstract

Fallout of long-lived radioactivity from nuclear bomb detonations is illustrated by a paper exercise conducted in 1959 involving about 4,000 megatons of nuclear explosives. The local fallout, that is the deposition taking place within a few days of the explosions, results in much of the U.S. being covered by Strontium-90 deposition in excess of about 400 millicuries per square kilometer. Some of the land areas of the Northern Hemisphere with heavier rainfall, those favorable for agriculture, also receive Strontium-90 deposition in excess of about 400 millicuries per square kilometer from delayed fallout months to years after the explosion. This delayed fallout would be deposited on neutral countries as well as combatants.

### Introduction

Two factors primarily distinguish nuclear devices from conventional explosives as instruments of war: first, the tremendous power derived from a small volume or mass and second, their radioactivity. Experience from the era of atmospheric testing of nuclear devices decades ago (Machta, 1963) provides the basic data for the patterns of behavior of the radioactivity, transport, and deposition of nuclear test debris as discussed in this chapter.

The fission products resulting from fission weapons and the fusion products, if the device is thermonuclear, are both gaseous and particulates. The particles, many of which form from delayed condensation, come in many sizes such that some will be deposited quickly, say within a day or less, to those so fine that they can remain airborne for years (Bleeker, 1961). This spectrum of particle fallout speeds combined with the vertical structure of the atmosphere has led analysts to distinguish three characteristic types of radioactive deposition, or fallout.

The first comprises those particles which are deposited within hours to perhaps a day. Generally having the least time for dispersion and hence dilution and still containing short-lived radioactivity, the quick fallout can be almost immediately lethal. It is the type against which one is advised to seek protection by shielding beneath a thick layer of soil. The distance downwind of the detonation to which such sheltering is advised can be up to several hundred kilometers and covers thousands of square kilometers. Aside from saying that the direction and distance from the detonation point of the lethal radioactivity area depends on the local winds, there is little to add since local fallout has been the subject of extensive discussions (e.g., Duffield and von Hipple, chapter 2). Its direct potential danger far exceeds that of delayed fallout.

The second category represents those particles small enough to remain suspended for at least a few days but injected after the explosion in the troposphere. The troposphere is the layer of the atmosphere in which our weather takes place and typically extends to heights of about 12 kilometers or so in temperate latitudes. Experience from the earlier nuclear testing period suggests that the dominant removal or deposition mechanism is precipitation scavenging. Since it rains or snows over land areas more in agricultural regions, a disproportionate amount of the radioactivity can be deposited on crops or agricultural soils and thus represents a continuous hazard through the food chain system (e.g., Bondietti, 1983).

For nuclear devices detonated near the ground but having a total energy yield of about 50 kilotons or more, some of the radioactivity and entrained ground level debris will enter the stratosphere, the atmospheric layer above the troposphere, (Peterson, 1970). Weather clouds rarely penetrate into the stratosphere so there is little or no precipitation scavenging at those heights. However, air movements will ultimately transfer the radioactive debris back to the troposphere where precipitation scavenging can again become effective. Larger particles injected initially into the stratosphere can settle down in close-in fallout. The stratospheric particles can also be deposited worldwide but not uniformly and it is this type of fallout which shall be discussed at greatest length. It is clear that both attackers and attacked, as well as neutrals, would be the beneficiaries of this "heavenly" deposit.

## Background

External gamma radiation or "shine" from particles and gases in the air as well as that deposited on the ground is the main source of damage of the close-in fallout. At later times for the tropospheric and stratospheric fallout, the rates of fallout are greatly reduced. The deposition on crops or accumulation on soils in which crops are grown adds to the amounts of radioactivity from local fallout available for human intake.

Fig. 3-1 represents an estimate of the base and top of the body of the nuclear mushroom which occurs in the temperate zone, that is, between about 30° and 60° where most of the likely military targets might occur (derived from Peterson, 1970). A further discussion of the estimated heights of the top and bottom of the bomb cloud, as a function of bomb yield, is given in Chang and Wuebbles, chapter 4, this volume. For purposes of the present discussion it is important to note that for explosions with a total yield of over about one megaton equivalent TNT, much of the cloud rises into the stratosphere. For heights of detonation well above the ground surface, even more of the nuclear cloud mass would initially penetrate into the stratosphere than is shown in Fig. 3-1.

## Close-in Fallout

The location of the downwind close-in fallout depends on the horizontal winds transporting the

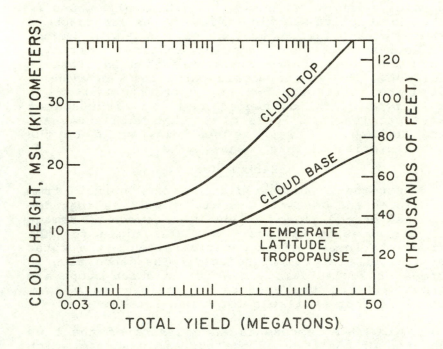

Fig. 3-1. An empirical model providing the "mushroom cap" cloud top and base as a function of the total yield or explosive power of the nuclear bomb for a detonation taking place at mid-latitudes near the surface of the earth.

falling particles. Typically, mid-latitude winds in the troposphere blow from west to east, but sometimes with strong north-south components. The speeds are also different from day to day and from season to season, being stronger generally in winter and spring than summer or fall. In the stratosphere, the mid-latitude winds are generally westerly during the winter and easterly during the summer. This stratospheric wind reversal is often referred to as the stratospheric monsoon system.

A fallout pattern for a possible attack on the U.S. is discussed below. Analogous patterns for the U.S. and Europe based on somewhat different nuclear bombing scenarios are discussed by Advisers (1982). The resulting distributions are quite similar.

The fallout picture, in Fig. 3-2, appears in the Congressional Hearings held in June 1959 based on winds of 17 October 1958 (U.S. Government, 1959, p. 56).

The assumed nuclear attack on the U.S. involved about 1,400 megatons derived from some 263 surface explosions. About 80 percent of the Strontium-90, the fission product we will mainly discuss, is deposited as local fallout, the distribution being as shown in Fig. 3-2. The Strontium-90 deposition can be converted to external gamma dose from short-lived radioactivity with the assumption that one roentgen per hour referenced to one hour is equivalent to 100 millicuries per square mile (39 millicuries per square kilometer) of Strontium-90. The figure shows that the unshaded areas with number "1" reflects Strontium-90 deposition greater than 1,000 millicuries per square mile. The lightly shaded areas with numbers "10" and covering much of the U. S. contain radiation concentrations between 10,000 and 100,000 millicuries per square mile. The very dark areas near the points of explosion contain dose rates equivalent to 100,000 to 300,000 millicuries per square mile.

An estimate can be given of the damage predicted from the attack scenario whose Strontium-90 fallout appears in Fig. 3-2 (U.S. Government, 1959, pp. 843-858). The damage is produced by blast, heat, direct radiation, and close-in fallout. In New York City, where two 10 megaton bombs

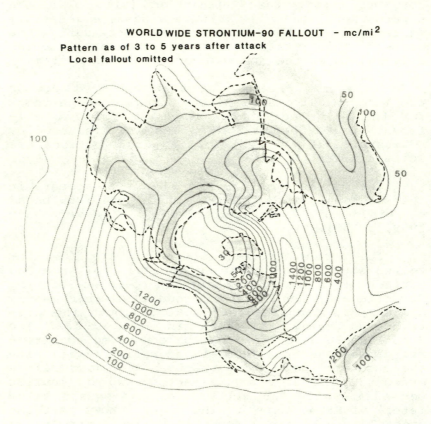

WORLD WIDE STRONTIUM-90 FALLOUT – mc/mi$^2$
Pattern as of 3 to 5 years after attack
Local fallout omitted

Fig. 3-2. Close-in or early Strontium-90 deposition from 263 hypothetical nuclear ground bursts of mixed fission-fusion weapons of various sizes plus delayed worldwide fallout (see Fig. 3-3). The bulk of the deposition of fission products in this figure is derived from the close-in fallout. To convert to Cesium-137 fallout, multiply the number for Strontium-90 deposition by about a factor of two.

were assumed to fall, half the population would be killed on either the first day or later from fatal injuries. For the twelve largest metropolitan areas in the U.S., only about 30 percent of the inhabitants would avoid injury or death. Nationally over 40 million people would die from the attack and only about 17 million would remain alive but injured. Of the latter, 10 million would have received radiaton doses from close-in fallout. Of the 41 million dwellings in 1959, 45 percent would be damaged by blast and another 18 million would receive close-in fallout which, without decontamination, would make them uninhabitable for at least 60 days. Thus, the damage to people and property from blast, heat, direct radiation, and close-in fallout from 263 bombs with a total megatonnage of less than 1,500 megatons of TNT falling on targets in the U.S. would create an unimaginable horror.

Strontium-90 has a half life of almost 30 years and a reasonably large fission yield. In the human body it behaves like calcium and thus concentrates in bone and bone marrow to which it delivers the main dose even though it is only a beta emitter. Cesium-137, a gamma emitter, with about the same half life as Strontium-90, behaves like potassium thus concentrating in muscle tissue. For all practical purposes, one may just about double the values of the labels on the isolines of Strontium-90 to estimate the deposition of Cesium-137 in Figs. 3-2 and 3-3. That is, where the Strontium-90 deposition might be predicted as say 1,000 millicuries per square mile, there would also be almost 20,000 millicuries per square mile of Cesium-137.

The deposition numbers for Strontium-90 in Figs. 2-3 and 3-3 for hemispheric fallout mean very little. Their conversion to human or ecological damage is necessary. But unfortunately this conversion process, involving as it does the weathering of radioisotopes in soil, the ability of crops to take up fission products falling on their leaves or accumulated in the soil, medical issues like retention of fission products in the body, linearity or thresholds of dose-response, and synergistic effects makes the conversion very complex. In fact, not many authors have been willing to predict, for example, the number of extra leukemia cases from the deposition numbers

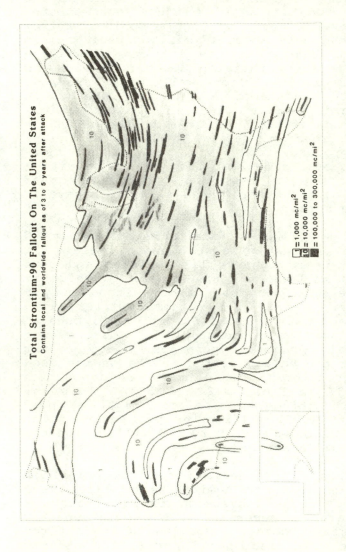

Total Strontium-90 Fallout On The United States
Contains local and worldwide fallout as of 3 to 5 years after attack

☐ = 1,000 mc/mi²
☒ = 10,000 mc/mi²
▓ = 100,000 to 300,000 mc/mi²

Fig. 3-3.  Worldwide accumulated and decayed Strontium-90 fallout from about 4,000 megatons of nuclear explosives with a 50-50 fission-fusion ratio detonated near the earth's surface in the temperate and near temperate latitudes.  The numbers represent the maximum accumulation which occurs about 3 to 5 years after the period of the detonations.

(National Academy of Sciences, 1975). It is suggested that eating crops grown with about 1,000 millicuries per square mile shown in Figs. 3-2 and 3-3 would increase the number of leukemia deaths by several tens of thousands in a population of 200 million people (U.S. Government, 1959, pp. 436-471). This number is subject to a very great uncertainty and according to recent estimates may be too low by a factor of as much as 30 (see, for instance, Coggle and Lindop, 1982; Upton, chapter 5).

Large areas of the U.S. would continue to contain long-lived radioactivity, numbers like 1,000 millicuries per square mile, even long after the external gamma radiation from local fallout died away allowing people to come out of their shelters and even if there were no subsequent fallout.

Note that even if agricultural areas are not themselves military targets, they still receive much fallout because of atmospheric transport. Further, although neither Mexico nor Canada were targeted in the exercise described above, they are not spared the fallout. Winds on a different day might well bring much more radioactivity to Canada or Mexico than shown here.

Thus, in addition to the death- and sick-producing shorter-lived fission products of close-in fallout normally publicized, there would also be a protracted period when foodstuffs are con-taminated in the attacked country and even in neighboring countries.

## Tropospheric and Stratospheric Fallout

In the 1959 exercise, in addition to the 1,400 megatons of nuclear explosives falling on the U. S., another 2,500 megatons were assumed to explode elsewhere in the temperate zone. All explosives were assumed to partition 50-50 between fission and fusion energy in the devices. It was also assumed that 5 percent of Strontium-90 is deposited as tropospheric fallout and the remaining 15 percent as stratospheric fallout.

One of the surprising meteorological findings, derived from measurements of radioactive fallout during the period of atmospheric tests

73

conducted some 20 to 30 years ago, was the timing and distribution of the stratospheric fallout component (Machta, 1957). One could be reasonably sure that it was stratospheric if the fallout occurred at least 2 or 3 months after a test series and it was known that the explosions were powerful enough to inject radioactive material into the stratosphere.

First, the greatest stratospheric fallout was found in the spring or early summer season. Second, it did not seem to matter very much whether the tests took place at Eniwetok and Bikini of the tropical North Pacific Ocean or in the high latitude Soviet Proving Grounds. In each case the temperate latitudes appeared to receive the greatest fallout. This is a consequence of the large scale meridional transport in the stratosphere and eventual transport of radioactive particles into the mid-latitude troposphere where they are eventually involved in rainout processes.

The worldwide isolines of predicted Strontium-90 deposition in units of millicuries per square mile is shown in Fig. 3-3. The fallout pattern represents the distillation of experience from the atmospheric testing period. Note that the pattern represents only the tropospheric and stratospheric deposition which has accumulated on the ground, crops, sea surface, etc., after about 3 to 5 years. The deposition from the troposphere occurs in a matter of months or less. But stratospheric fallout tapers off approximately exponentially with a mean time constant of a little less than 2 years. Thus, even after 3 to 5 years following the war, more long-lived fission products will be settling to earth. But after about 3 to 5 years, the decay of the two main isotopes, Strontium-90 and Cesium-137 on the ground, will balance or exceed the additional fallout.

The predicted fallout distribution shown in Fig. 3-3 reflects the greater average deposition in temperate zones and the geographical differences where it rains or snows. The latter is the reason for the higher expected deposition of the stormy North Atlantic and the northern Pacific Ocean. The amount of Strontium-90 even in the highest regions fall below most of the deposition in the close-in patterns of Fig. 3-2. But there is a sizeable agricultural area in which the accumulated Strontium-90 exceeds 1,000 millicuries per square mile from this particular assumption of 4,000 megatons of nuclear explosives. It will be recalled that eating food contaminated with this much Strontium-90 radiation might well result in an additional 20,000 or more cases of leukemia in an area with a 200 million population like the U.S., Western Europe, or the Soviet Union.

This predicted pattern of delayed fallout would remain essentially unchanged irrespective of the detailed location of the theater of war unless it moved to the Southern Hemisphere. It would, however, be scaled up or down depending on the amount of fission products available for delayed fallout. Since the hypothesized attack involves detonations at the ground already resulting in 80 percent local Strontium-90 fallout, there is no way short of using cleaner bombs for significantly reducing the numbers on this picture if 4,000 megatons are exploded.

The above discussion dealt with the easy part of predicting the consequences of delayed fallout from a nuclear war. What goes up must come down and it is only a matter of predicting where and when the fallout occurs. But nonmeteorological uncertainties such as medical damage are very much larger. However, unless the harm to man or his environment almost entirely disappears, any casualty numbers are usually so unacceptable to the public that the uncertainties are irrelevant.

Although one can envisage arguments for making the amount of delayed fallout and its consequences either lesser or greater than we have seen in this chapter, it is worth mentioning some of the reasons why it is more likely to be much worse. First, there are other fission products in the delayed fallout that will add to man's insult beyond Strontium-90 or Cesium-137. The 8-day Iodine-131 can find its way to the thyroids of those persons, especially, who drink fresh milk (List et al., 1964). A small additional dose to the bone and bone marrow will arise from the ingestion of 50-day Strontium-89. Inhalation and ingestion of plutonium isotopes of very long half lives and other mixed fission products will add to man's irradiation from delayed fallout causing somatic, genetic, and life-shortening effects. Carbon-14, a 5560-year fusion bomb product, will become part of the human protoplasm for hundreds of generations and slowly impose genetic damage.

With regard to the fallout patterns given in Figs. 3-2 and 3-3, these too, are likely underestimates. All the detonations in the 1959 exercise took place at ground level leaving a minimum amount of radioactivity for the worldwide delayed fallout. A war with air bursts and the same megatonnage would greatly increase the delayed fallout. Second, the size of the nuclear war, 4,000 megatons, is closer to the low end of the scale, 5,000 to 10,000 megatons, suggested for the Ambio Reference Scenario exercises (Advisors, 1982). Finally, in reality the smooth isolines in both Figs. 3-2 and 3-3 would become irregular with isolated hot spots as was seen from fallout in the 1950s and 1960s. Some areas would therefore receive much higher fallout than shown.

## Conclusions

It is clear that this discussion has emphasized long-term, worldwide aspects of radioactive fallout. The short-term close-in fallout is, by far, the most immediately dangerous and lethal consequences of a nuclear war. But, that occurs mainly on the soil of an enemy of the attacker and might be viewed as an added advantage in the war.

But, if the attacker hopes to benefit from the agricultural produce of the attacked nation as a spoil of war, the foodstuffs will be as undesirable to him as it would be to the survivors of the attack.

The delayed fallout will increase health risks to all countries in the temperate and near temperate zones including neutrals. This delayed fallout is somewhat analogous to the insult from ozone depletion and climate change that might be produced by a nuclear war in that it affects a much wider population (Turco et al., 1983; Ehrlich et al., 1983; Chang and Wuebbles, chapter 4). But while there may be doubts about the theories of the destruction of the ozone layers or creating a new climate regime, there are no doubts about the reality of delayed fallout even if we have trouble understanding its full significance.

76

Herman Kahn in the 1959 Congressional Hearings thought the "backlash" from the delayed radioactivity would deter very little or none at all. On the other hand, the public uproar in the 1950s about fallout from atmospheric nuclear testing on both sides of the Iron Curtain, with much less fallout than in current scenarios of a nuclear war, contributed to the pressures for the signing of the ban on atmospheric tests by the major powers. The worldwide fallout consequences of a nuclear war should also be considered in formulating public policy.

## References

Advisers, 1982: Reference scenario: how a nuclear war might be fought, Ambio XI, 94-99.

Bleeker, W., 1961: Meteorological Factors Influencing the Transport and Removal of Radioactive Debris, World Meteorological Organization Technical Note 43, Geneva.

Bondietti, E. A., 1982: Effects on agriculture, Ambio XI, 138-142.

Coggle, J. E. and P. J. Lindop, 1982: Medical consequences of radiation following a global nuclear war, Ambio XI, 106-113.

Ehrlich, P. R., J. Harte, M. A. Harwell, P. H. Raven, C. Sagan, G. M. Woodwell, J. Berry, E. S. Ayensu, A. H. Ehrlich, T. Eisner, S. J. Gould, H. D. Grover, R. Herrera, R. M. May, E. Mayr, C. P. McKay, H. A. Mooney, N. Meyers, D. Pimental, J. M. Teal, 1983: Long-term biological consequences of nuclear war, Science, 222, 1293-1300.

List, R. J., K. Telegadas, and G. J. Ferber, 1964: Meteorological evaluation of the sources of iodine-131 in pasteurized milk, Science, 146, 59-64.

Machta, L., 1957: Some applications of radioactive tracers in meteorology,Ann. of the Inter. Geophys. Year, Part V, Nuclear Radiation (Part II), 313-324.

Machta, L., 1963: Worldwide radioactive fallout from nuclear tests - Part I, Nuclear Safety 4, 103-111, Part II, 5, 95-104.

National Academy of Sciences, 1975: Long term worldwide effects of multiple nuclear-weapon detonations, Washington, D. C.

Peterson, K., 1970: An empirical model for estimating worldwide deposition from atmospheric nuclear detonations, Health Phys., 18, 357-378.

Turco, R. P., O. B. Toon, T. P. Ackerman, J. B. Pollack, C. Sagan, 1983: Nuclear winter: global consequences of multiple nuclear explosions, Science, 222, 1283-1292.

U.S. Government, 1959: Biological and Environmental Effects of Nuclear War, Hearings before the Special Subcommittee on Radiation of the Joint Committee on Atomic Energy, 86th Congress.

*Julius S. Chang, Donald J. Wuebbles*

# 4. Nuclear Explosions and Atmospheric Ozone

### Abstract

Ever since the first atmospheric nuclear test in New Mexico, scientists have been concerned with the potential atmospheric impact of such a violent man-made event. The environmental impacts range from the earlier concern over possible nuclear ignition of the whole atmosphere, to global dispersion of radionuclides, to the destruction of the atmospheric layer, to the climatic consequences of dust and aerosol loading from nuclear war.

Among the potential global effects of nuclear war, significant destruction of the stratospheric ozone layer is the most easily studied. During the past decade, there have been important advances in understanding atmospheric chemistry and transport processes, and the suggested reduction of the stratospheric ozone concentration can be realistically evaluated. Current theory (models) indicates that a full-scale nuclear exchange of about 10,000 Mt between the U.S. and the USSR could result in more than a 50 percent destruction of the earth's protective ozone layer. Such drastic changes can persist for many years. The assumptions used in the theoretical calculations and impacts of the inherent uncertainties of all such analyses that are based on computational modeling are discussed.

## Introduction

A nuclear explosion is without question the most violent single act ever invented by man. Nuclear weapons are designed for their overwhelming military effectiveness. Not much attention has been devoted to the potential geophysical consequences of a large number of atmospheric nuclear explosions. For obvious reasons, only the direct effects—blast, fire,and radiation—are of interest to the military planners. Among these, only radioactivity was thought to have a long-term environmental impact. During the past decade, advances in the atmospheric sciences have led to the discovery of several new concerns, namely, the possibility of destroying the earth's protective ozone layer and altering the climate. Current theory suggests that a large number of atmospheric nuclear explosions can produce enough nitrogen oxides, loft enough dust, and createenough smoke from urban and wild fires to significantly alter the physical and chemical structures of the atmosphere for periods ranging from months to years. Although these possibilities are concurrent events and no overall system analysis has been carried out for any hypothetical scenario, all the principal mechanisms have been studied individually. The available results strongly suggest that nuclear confrontation is truly global in scope. The spread in radioactive debris, the change in the amount of solar radiation reaching the earth's surface, and the surface temperature and other climatic variables occur everywhere. Although the extend of local effects will be different, it can be safely said that there will be no unaffected neutral bystanders. Therefore, the scientific credibility of these potential geophysical consequences can have far-reaching influences in national and international decision-making processes.

Among the potential global effects of nuclear war, the destruction of the atmospheric ozone layer is the most easily studied in the open literature. The study of radioactivity from nuclear war depends very much upon the design details of the individual weapons. Such information is usually not available in the open literature. The study of the climatic impact of dust, aerosol, and smoke from nuclear war requires, among other

80

things, detailed knowledge of targeting philoso-
phies and the fire propagation characteristics of
forests and modern cities. Again, this information is not easily available. However, ozone
destruction theory depends mostly upon knowledge
of thermo-energy release, i.e., the total yield of
individual weapons. Of course, there are many
other important factors such as atmospheric transport, pollutant removal and scavenging, chemical
transformation and interactions, and atmospheric
radiative transfer processes. Most of these are
common to all of the above-mentioned effect
studies. The level of significance varies among
the studies.

This chapter summarizes some recent calculations on the effects of nuclear war on atmospheric
ozone. We begin with a short historical note on
the evolving interest in this problem. We next
discuss the physical and chemical processes leading to ozone reduction after hypothetical atmospheric nuclear exchanges. The current status of
estimated ozone changes is then presented. Finally, we explore the assumptions used in the theoretical calculation of ozone destruction from
nuclear war and discuss the impact of the inherent
uncertainties of the input variables and modeling
techniques.

## Historical Notes

As early as the first nuclear test at
Alamogordo, New Mexico (1945), there has been concern over the potential atmospheric effect of
atmospheric nuclear explosions. Konopinski and
Teller (1943) carried out a short analysis of the
possibility of accidentally initiating self-
propagating nuclear burning of the atmosphere.
They concluded that it is impossible to do so.
Several other more refined studies came to the
same conclusion (Konopinski et al., 1946; Bethe,
1946; Weaver and Wood, 1979). A Lawrence
Livermore National Laboratory internal memo by
Bonner (1971) is apparently the first documented
concern over the effects of nitrogen oxides from
nuclear tests on the ozone concentration in the
stratosphere. Based on the then available and
limited data, Bonner concluded that no significant
effect can be expected from past atmospheric

nuclear tests. However, he only considered the possible effect of individual explosion and the not the cumulative impact. Foley and Ruderman (1973) were the first to study the potential cumulative effect of atmospheric test series in the late 1950s and early 1960s, mainly by the U.S. and the USSR. Their study was further expanded and refined by Johnston et al., (1973) and Goldsmith et al. (1973). A detailed analysis of most of the important physical parameters and input variables with special emphasis on the uncertainties in the chemical kinetics database was published by Chang et al. (1979). The principal conclusion was that, although stratospheric ozone was expected to be affected by the past tests, the past ozone record is not adequate in detecting the small signal.

Hampson (1974) published the first discussion on the potential damage to the ozone layer after a large number of nuclear exchanges. At about the same time, others had also begun similar studies. The reports by the National Academy of Sciences, (1975), MacCracken and Chang (1975), and Whitten et al. (1975) all concluded that nuclear exchanges in the range of 10,000 Mt can severely reduce the stratospheric ozone layer over a period of several years. An unpublished report by Duewer et al. (1978) included the first parametric study on the effects of different individual weapon yields and effective stratospheric residence times. It was found that the then changing understanding of chemical kinetics rate coefficients did not alter the principal conclusion of the earlier reports. A 1979 Office of Technology Assessment report (Office of Technology Assessment, 1979) came to different conclusions without furnishing any technical details. More recently, the articles and book by Schell (1982) and, more notably, the work of Crutzen and Birks (1982) have stimulated wide interest both in the scientific community and society as a whole. The work of Crutzen and Birks raised new scientific concerns, particulary the climatic consequences of dust and smoke from nuclear explosions. They also considered the ozone question, but with a very different scenario than was assumed in the past. They only performed limited calculations involving large weapons. Their results will be compared to our results later.

## Atmospheric Nuclear Explosions and Ozone

The high temperature environment created by an atmospheric nuclear explosion can mix and heat a large volume of air to such temperatures so as to produce significant amounts of nitrogen oxides ($NO_x$). This volume of hot gas can rise high up into the atmosphere. If the individual explosion is sufficiently large, the hot cloud could reach well into the stratosphere where the entrained NO molecules can add to the natural ozone destruction processes leading to a net decrease in stratospheric ozone. Depending upon the total amount of NO molecules so introduced, the resulting ozone decrease will lead to a temperature decrease in the stratosphere and an increase in solar ultraviolet radiation received at the surface. Because of the normally weak transport processes between the stratosphere and troposphere, the stratospheric ozone decrease and consequent increase in solar ultraviolet radiation at the earth's surface are expected to last for several years. Such changes would then lead to significant long-term human health, agricultural, and general ecological changes (National Research Council, 1983). A full-scale nuclear exchange among the superpowers in the energy range of a few thousand to more than ten thousand equivalent megatons of nuclear explosions can certainly produce enough NO molecules. Furthermore, if a sufficient number of large (greater than 0.5 Mt) individual warheads is used, enough of these NO molecules will reach stratospheric heights, hence the ozone destruction and other consequences.

Although a detailed consideration of the full problem based on well-understood physical and chemical processes is still beyond the computing power of existing technology, this problem can be analyzed through the natural separation of time scales for the major physical processes. The physical processes leading to ozone changes can be roughly separated into four stages: NO production from atmospheric nuclear explosions, nuclear cloud stabilization in the stratosphere, $NO_x$ catalytic ozone destruction, and pollutant dispersion and removal. Of course, there are many detailed mechanisms occurring within each of these stages, and many others such as all the photochemical interactions which occur throughout the atmospheric life cycle of the pollutants. For the nuclear war

scenario, only a few dominant processes occur
during each of the four stages. The initial production of NO molecules takes place within a few
minutes after the explosion. During this time,
very few of the other major processes have any impact. The hot gas cloud would then rise into the
stratosphere in about ten minutes or so. The
chemical interactions in the stratosphere are such
that, if we are only interested in the global
ozone balance, there is no need to know the detailed mix of chemical species in the hot cloud.
The critical information is the total amount of
$NO_x$, i.e., various forms of nitrogen-containing
molecules except $N_2$. After reaching the stabilization altitude, the excess $NO_x$ in the nuclear
cloud then mixes with the ambient air and inter-
acts with the various forms of oxygen molecules.
This mixture will reach a new state of equilibrium
within a few minutes to a few hours. The subsequent global dispersion occurs at such a slow pace
that the chemical system can always maintain a
reasonable state of quasi-equilibrium. It was
first pointed out by Foley and Ruderman (1973)
that approximately one third of the total explosion yield goes to heat the nuclear cloud. The
rest of the energy dissipates as a direct blast
wave and radiation. Depending upon the efficiency
of the mixing processes with surrounding air,
there is uncertainty in the number of NO molecules
produced per megaton nuclear yield by a factor of
four (Gilmore, 1975) to six (Johnston et al.,
1973), with a mean of approximately $0.9 \times 10^{32}$
molecules per megaton yield. If one considers
some detrainment of the stem of the mushroom cloud
during its rise, as suggested by the COMESA (1975)
report, then a reasonable $NO_x$ production rate
would be $0.7 \times 10^{32}$ molecules/Mt. The extent of
mixing and detrainment is not well known, and this
number is uncertain by at least a factor of two.
In any case, the calculated ozone reduction is essentially a linear function of this number.

One of the more interesting questions in this
area of research is the cloud stabilization process. There is very little current information on
the complex dynamic processes establishing the
proper height a given hot cloud can reach. The
best available information came from past U.S.
Pacific tests. Very little reliable information
came from past USSR tests. Foley and Ruderman
(1973) gave a parameterization for the top and

84

bottom of the stabilized cloud versus explosion yield as:

$$CT \text{ (km)} = 22Y^{0.2}, \text{ and } CB \text{ (km)} = 13Y^{0.2},$$

where CT and CB are the cloud top and cloud bottom heights, respectively. Y is the total nuclear yield in megaton TNT equivalent. Other estimates of cloud heights from past nuclear tests are given by, for instance, Seitz et al., (1968), Telegadas and List (1969), and Martell (1970) (see, also, Machta, chapter 3). Chang et al. (1979) summarize the available information and discuss the significance of the differences. For relatively low yield explosions, all the estimates of cloud stabilization heights are approximately the same. For yields above one megaton, the above estimates of cloud tops and bottoms are a little higher than the others (at most by a few km). The above estimates result in a larger initial amount of ozone destruction when compared to the others. We shall adopt the above expressions as the best available estimates for near-surface explosions.

The natural chemical cycles leading to the production and destruction of stratospheric ozone have been under intensive study for the past decade. The naturally abundant $O_2$ molecules are dissociated by absorption of short wavelength solar radiation into two oxygen atoms which can then recombine with $O_2$ to form ozone ($O_3$). This production mechanism is partially balanced by the loss through O and $O_3$ recombination to form two $O_2$ molecules. Crutzen (1971) and Johnston (1971) found that the catalytic cycle

$$
\begin{aligned}
NO + O_3 &\rightarrow NO_2 + O_2 \\
NO_2 + O &\rightarrow NO + O_2 \\
\hline
\text{Net:} \quad O + O_3 &\rightarrow O_2 + O_2
\end{aligned}
$$

is the most dominant loss mechanism for ozone (or, more precisely, the odd-oxygens, O and $O_3$) in the stratosphere. Other equivalent catalytic cycles involving HO and $HO_2$ or Cl and ClO pairs are also found to be important (e.g., Climatic Impact Assessment Program (1975) and World Meteorological Organization (1981)). The additional amount of NO and $NO_2$ introduced by the nuclear cloud can significantly enhance the odd-oxygen loss rate, resulting in a decrease in ozone. Current theory of atmospheric chemistry shows a considerable degree of non-linear interaction among many chemical spe-

85

cies. None of the above-mentioned catalytical
cycles acts independently of the others. There
are many so-called transfer reactions which convert particular molecules from one group of reac-
tants to others. Modern models of stratospheric
chemistry usually consider thirty to fifty individual species involving more than one hundred chemical and photochemical reactions. World Meteorological Organization (1981) contains a good summary of the current evaluated chemical database
used in most calculations involving stratospheric
chemistry.

Detailed analysis of coupled transport and
chemical processes in the atmosphere would require
the use of three-dimensional models. Unfortunately, even the largest and fastest of the current
generation of computers is not able to meet the
computing needs of this type of model. There is
as of yet no three-dimensional model with detailed
consideration of chemical interactions. Almost
all current models of stratospheric chemistry use
one form of parameterized transport or another,
whether the model is one-dimensional (vertical
transport only) or two-dimensional (vertical and
meridional). Studies by Chang (1974), Hunten
(1975), Chang et al. (1979), and others clarify
the sensitivity of the chemical models to the
transport parameters. A level of uncertainty is
inherent within these parameterizations which may
only be reduced through the future use of three-
dimensional models. For the present type of
study, Chang et al. (1979) found that the modeling
results are most sensitive to the uncertainties of
the chemical kinetics reaction coefficients.

Briefly, all the current models consist of a
set of continuity equations describing the conservation of individual chemical species. A typical equation is:

$$\frac{\partial c_i}{\partial t} = - \nabla \cdot F_i + P_i - L_i + S_i \, ,$$

where $c_i$ if the concentration of the ith constituent expressed in terms of molecules/cm$^3$/sec,
t is time, $F_i$ is the transport flux of the ith
constituent, $P_i$ and $L_i$ are the chemical and
photochemical production and loss rates of $c_i$,
respectively, and $S_i$ represents all other

ources and sinks such as the pollutants from
uclear explosions or other chemicals released at
he earth's surface. The exact form of the tran-
port flux depends upon the dimensionality and the
esign objective of the model. Given a set of in-
ut conditions, the full system is then solved
umerically on a computer. For the present con-
ideration, the inputs are the natural (unperturb-
d) atmosphere, the injection height parameteri-
ations, the $NO_x$ production rate, the transport
arameterization, and the hypothetical nuclear war
cenario, including the total yield and the mix of
ndividual weapon yields.

Hypothetical Scenarios and
Atmospheric Ozone Changes

There are many ways we may construct a set of
ypothetical nuclear war scenarios. The recent
pecial issue of Ambio (1982) contains a very de-
ailed construct of a possible scenario. For our
urposes, only a rough estimate will be required.
'e are only interested in a global estimate of the
zone reduction, not in local or even regional-
cale reductions. The chemical model used is not
apable of handling finer geophysical details.

A recent study by the Congressional Research
ervice (1982) estimates that, under the current
ALT II guidelines, the U.S. and USSR stockpiles
f strategic nuclear weapons will be significantly
ifferent from earlier estimates of the Office of
echnology Assessment (1979). In addition to dif-
erences in total yields (13,444 megatons (Office
f Technology Assessment) vs. 10,606 megatons
Congressional Research Service)), there are large
ifferences in deployed weapons systems (see
ables 4-1 and 4-2). We considered six hypotheti-
al scenarios for both sets of estimated stock-
iles:

a) all-out exchange, all weapons successfully detonated;
b) only half of each type weapon is successfully detonated;
c) only weapons with individual yields
   greater than 0.8 Mt are used;
d) only weapons with individual yields less
   than or equal to 0.8 Mt are used;
e) USSR stockpile only;
f) U.S. stockpile only.

1

87

Table 4-1

An Estimate of 1983 Inventory of Deployed
Strategic Offensive Weapons (Congressional
Research Service, 1982)

|  | Number of Warheads | Yield per Warhead (Mts) | Subtotal Yield (Mts) |
|---|---|---|---|
| USSR | 58 | 20 | 1,160 |
|  | 60 | 10 | 600 |
|  | 32 | 6 | 190 |
|  | 313 | 1.0 | 313 |
|  | 518 | 0.95 | 492.1 |
|  | 1,200 | 0.9 | 1,080 |
|  | 286 | 0.8 | 228.8 |
|  | 542 | 0.75 | 406.5 |
|  | 304 | 0.7 | 212.8 |
|  | 60 | 0.6 | 36 |
|  | 2,800 | 0.55 | 1,540 |
|  | 2,280 | 0.2 | 456 |
| U.S. | 1,524 | 1.2 | 1,828.8 |
|  | 2,736 | 0.4 | 1,094.4 |
|  | 900 | 0.335 | 301.5 |
|  | 612 | 0.2 | 122.4 |
|  | 1,944 | 0.17 | 330.48 |
|  | 2,112 | 0.1 | 211.2 |
|  |  | Total | 10,605.98 |

(Use of these estimates is for illustrative purposes only, and this use does not confirm nor deny
the validity of the reference cited.)

Table 4-2

An Estimate of Strategic Nuclear Forces in 1985
(Office of Technology Assessment, 1979)

|       | Number of Warheads | Yield per Warhead (Mts) | Subtotal Yield (Mts) |
|-------|--------------------|-------------------------|----------------------|
| USSR  | 100                | 20                      | 2,000                |
|       | 40                 | 5                       | 200                  |
|       | 2,794              | 1.5                     | 4,191                |
|       | 660                | 1.0                     | 660                  |
|       | 3,000              | 0.8                     | 2,400                |
|       | 800                | 0.6                     | 480                  |
|       | 900                | 0.2                     | 180                  |
|       |                    |                         |                      |
| U.S.  | 54                 | 9                       | 486                  |
|       | 1,230              | 1.0                     | 1,230                |
|       | 4,410              | 0.2                     | 882                  |
|       | 1,650              | 0.17                    | 280.5                |
|       | 3,200              | 0.10                    | 320                  |
|       | 3,360              | 0.04                    | 134.4                |
|       |                    | Total                   | 13,443.9             |

(Use of these estimates is for illustrative purposes only, and this use does not confirm nor deny
the validity of the reference cited.)

As in Chang et al. (1979), all explosions were assumed to take place simultaneously, and the $NO_x$ is injected into the upper atmosphere according to the cloud stabilization height prescriptions for each warhead. There was no consideration of possible synergistic effects of multiple detonations of small-yield weapons in proximity to each other to possibly form an aggregate cloud comparable to larger-yield weapons. The cloud was further assumed to spread uniformly over the Northern Hemisphere with no further horizontal dilution due to transport into the Southern Hemisphere. This artifact of the calculation procedure would lead to a small initial underestimate of the Northern Hemispheric mid-latitude ozone decrease and larger decreases for the polar area. For the later estimates (a few years later), the Northern Hemisphere ozone as given here should be an overestimate. It is difficult to quantify these differences, but our one-dimensional model result is very similar to the two-dimensional result of Crutzen and Birks (1982). A major uncertainty in intermodel comparison is the lack of detailed information on the chemical system used. Chang et al. (1979) have shown that the major uncertainty in such calculations is the chemical rate coefficients used. Fortunately, the past decades of intensive information exchange among all the stratospheric modeling groups have assured us of the fundamental similarity of most of the models (World Meteorological Organization, 1981). Nevertheless, a detailed comparison may be desirable in the future for such an important application of the models.

In our study, the model estimated that ozone decreases for all six cases of the Congressional Research Service and the Office of Technology Assessment stockpiles are directly proportional to the source functions. This is mostly due to a broad mix of individual yields in both estimates of stockpiles and the fact that we are only looking at the hemispherically-averaged ozone decreases. Hereafter, we shall only discuss the six cases corresponding to the Congressional Research Service estimates. For the full exchange of 10,606 Mt, we estimate a peak Northern Hemispheric decrease of 51 percent, while Crutzen and Birks (1982) estimated a 65 percent decrease using 10,000 Mt of total yield in an equal mix of 1 and 5 Mt weapons. This is almost proportional to the difference in larger weapons for the Congressional Research Service estimates. A similar difference is in the estimates for mid-latitudes two years after the hypothetical event.

The time evolution of the ozone decreases for the six cases is shown in Figs. 4-1 and 4-2. It is seen that there is no significant difference in the time evolution of the effects from the previous National Academy of Sciences analysis (National Academy of Sciences, 1975). In all cases, maximum effects occur in about six months and decay to less than 10 percent total ozone reduction within five years. Due to a saturation effect of the chemical system, cutting the source by 50 percent (Case B) does not lead to a factor two less in effect. Most of the damage (as much as a 42 percent decrease out of a total of 51 percent) to the ozone layer is due to the high yield weapons, i.e., greater than 0.8 Mt individual yields (Case C). Although almost half of the total yields are in the less than or equal to 0.8 Mt individual yield range, they contribute less than 16 percent out of a total of 51 percent peak ozone decrease. This is mostly due to the low altitude of stabilization for these comparatively low yield weapons. The $NO_x$ injected at these altitudes participates in the well-known smog reactions leading to a small increase in upper tropospheric ozone that compensates the upper-level decrease (Case D). Finally, as far as total stratospheric ozone is concerned, the USSR stockpile is about twice as destructive as the U.S. stockpile (Fig. 4-2). It should be pointed out that insofar as the enhanced solar UV radiation at the earth's surface is a concern, the suggested tropospheric dust and smoke increase (Crutzen and Birks, 1982) may compensate for the decrease in ozone. However, this very much depends on the size distributions of the particulates. The duration of this compensating effect is expected to be short since the average residence time in the troposphere is about one to two orders of magnitude less than that in the stratosphere.

As was mentioned before, another effect of stratospheric ozone decrease is the reduced heating of the stratosphere. However, in this case, the overwhelming increase in $NO_x$ in the form of $NO_2$ by factors of 15 or more at 90 days after the event can actually lead to a local temperature in-

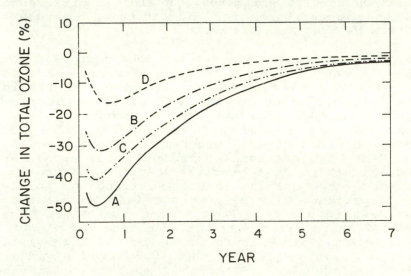

Fig. 4-1. Percent total ozone change in the
Northern Hemisphere for four different
hypothetical nuclear exchange scenarios.

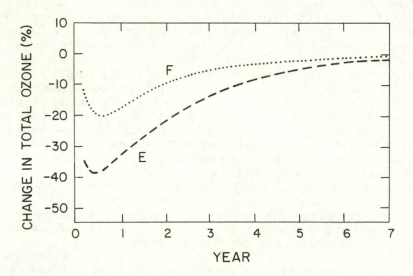

Fig. 4-2. Percent total ozone change in the
Northern Hemisphere for two different
hypothetical nuclear exchange scenarios.

crease. We estimated that there could be a 15 K increase in temperature around 25 km altitude with smaller increases at all levels reaching well into the upper stratosphere. At above 40 km, where the compensatory $NO_2$ heating is no longer effective, there is a small decrease of a few degrees. It is not clear how realistic these simple estimates of temperature change may be. More careful analysis using better dynamic models will be required in the future.

## References

Ambio, 1982: Nuclear war: the aftermath, Ambio, Xl, 76-176.

Bethe, H. A., 1946: Can air or water be exploded? Bull. Atom. Sci., 1, 2 and 14.

Bonner, N., 1971: Nitrogen oxides in the stratosphere from nuclear tests: effects on ozone concentration, Radiochem. Div., Lawrence Livermore Natl. Lab., Livermore, CA, 4 pp. (internal memo).

Chang, J. S., 1974: Simulations, perturbations, and interpretations. In Proc. of the Third CIAP Conference, DOT-TST-OST-74-15, U.S. Dept. of Transp., Boston, MA, 330-341.

Chang, J.S., W. H. Duewer, and D. J. Wuebbles, 1979: The atmospheric nuclear tests of the 1950s and 1960s: a possible test of ozone depletion theories, J. Geophys. Res., 84. 1755-1765.

Climatic Impact Assessment Program, 1975: The Stratosphere Perturbed by Propulsion Effluents, CIAP Monograph III, DOT-TST-75-53, U.S. Dept. of Transp., Washington, D.C.

COMESA, 1975: The Report of the Committee on Meteorological Effects of Stratospheric Aircraft (1972-1975), U.K. Meteorological Office, Bracknell, England.

Congressional Research Service, 1982: Private communication from Rep. A. Gore, Jr.

Crutzen, P. J., 1971: Ozone production rates in an oxygen-hydrogen-nitrogen oxide atmosphere, J. Geophys. Res., 76, 7311-7327.

Crutzen, P. J., and J. W. Birks, 1982: The atmosphere after a nuclear war: twilight at noon, Ambio, XI, 114-125.

Duewer, W. H., D. J. Wuebbles, and J. S. Chang, 1978: The effects of a massive pulse injection of $NO_x$ into the stratosphere,

LLNL Rep. No. UCRL-80397, Lawrence Livermore
Natl. Lab., Livermore, CA.

Foley, H. M., and M. A. Ruderman, 1973:
Stratospheric NO production from past nuclear
explosions, J. Geophys. Res., 78, 4441-4450.

Gilmore, F. R., 1975: The production of nitrogen
oxides by low-altitude nuclear explosions,
J. Geophys. Res., 80, 4553-4554.

Goldsmith, P., A. F. Tuck, J. S. Foot, E. L.
Simmons, and R. L. Newson, 1973: Nitrogen
oxides, nuclear weapon testing, Concorde, and
stratospheric ozone, Nature, 244, 545-551.

Hampson, J., 1974: Photochemical war on the
atmosphere, Nature, 250, 189-191.

Hunten, D. M., 1975: Estimates of stratospheric
pollution by an analytical model. In Proc.
of the U.S. Nat. Acad. Sci., Nat. Acad. Sci.,
Washington, D.C., 72, 4711-4715.

Johnston, H. S., 1971: Reduction of stratospheric
ozone by nitrogen oxide catalysts from
supersonic transport exhaust, Science, 173,
517-522.

Johnston, H. S., G. Whitten, and J. Birks, 1973:
Effects of nuclear explosions on
stratospheric nitric oxide and ozone, J.
Geophys. Res., 78, 6107-6135.

Konopinski, E. J., and E. Teller, 1943: Ignition
of the atmosphere, Los Alamos Natl. Lab., Los
Alamos, NM (unpublished paper).

Konopinski, E. J., C. Marvin, and E. Teller, 1946:
Ignition of the atmosphere with nuclear
bombs, Rep. No. LA-602, Los Alamos Natl.
Lab., Los Alamos, NM (unpublished paper).

MacCracken, M. C., and J. S. Chang, eds., 1975: A
preliminary study of the potential chemical
and climatic effects of atmospheric nuclear
explosions, LLNL Rep. No. UCRL-51653,
Lawrence livermore Natl. Lab., Livermore, CA.

Martell, E. A., 1970: Transport patterns and
residence times for atmospheric trace
constituents vs. altitude. In Radionuclides
in the Environment, E. C. Freeling, ed.,
Adv. in Chem., 93, 138-156.

National Academy of Sciences, 1975: Long-term
Worldwide Effects of Multiple Nuclear
Weapons, National Academy of Sciences Press,
Washington, D.C.

National Research Council, 1983: Causes and
Effects of Changes in Stratospheric Ozone:
Update 1983, Nat. Res. Coun., Washington,
D.C.

Office of Technology Assessment, 1979: The Effects of Nuclear War, Office of Technology Assessment, U.S. Congress, Washington, D.C.

Schell, J., 1982: Fate of the Earth, Knopf Publishing Co., New York, NY.

Seitz, H., B. Davidson, J. P. Friend, and H. W. Feely, 1968: Numerical models of transport diffusion and fallout of stratospheric radioactive materials, Final Report on Project Streak, USAEC Rep. No. NYO-3654-4, Atom. Energy Comm., Washington, D.C.

Telegadas, K., and R. J. List, 1969: Are particulate radioactive tracers indicative of stratospheric motions? J. Geophys. Res., 74, 1339-1350.

Weaver, T. A., and L. Wood, 1979: Necessary conditions for the initiation and propagation of nuclear-detonated waves in plane atmosphere, Phy. Rev. A., 20, 316-328.

Whitten, R. C., W. J. Borucki, and R. P. Turco, 1975: Possible ozone depletions following nuclear explosions, Nature, 257, 38-39.

World Meteorological Organization, 1981: The Stratosphere 1981: Theory and Measurements, World Meteorological Organization, Geneva, Switzerland.

( Work performed under the auspicies of the U.S. Department of Energy by the Lawrence Livermore Laboratory under contract W-7405-Eng-48. )

# 5. Radiation Effects on Humans

### Abstract

An analysis is presented of the health impacts of a full-scale nuclear war. Within the first weeks following the bomb explosions there could be on the order of tens of millions of fatalities. For the survivors, contained widespread fallout and disruption to normal health support systems would result in enormously increased illness and mortality including cancer and genetic disorders from exposure to ionizing radiation.

### Introduction

In considering the health impacts of nuclear weapons, one must take into account a broad spectrum of radiation effects. These include short-term effects such as prompt radiation sickness and death, and middle-term effects such as malnutrition and epidemics of infectious disease occurring over a period of two months to two years and long-term effects such as an increase in the incidence of cancer and genetic disease. This paper surveys the entire spectrum of such effects. It comments particularly on long-term effects, since other effects are discussed in part by Duffield and von Hippel, chapter 2.

To view the problem in perspective, one must recognize that some radiation effects require a dose thousands of times higher than natural background radiation levels of the magnitude estimated

Table 5-1

Estimates of Annual Whole-Body Radiation Doses to the U.S. Population

| Source of Radiation | Average Dose Rates (mSy/year)[a] |
|---|---|
| **Natural** | |
| Environmental | |
| Cosmic Radiation | 0.28 (28-130)[b] |
| Terrestrial Radiation | 0.26 (30-115)[c] |
| Internal Radioactive Isotopes | 0.26 |
| Subtotal | 0.80 |
| | |
| **Man-Made** | |
| Environmental | |
| Technologically Enhanced | 0.04 |
| Global Fallout | 0.04 |
| Nuclear Power | 0.002 |
| Medical | |
| Diagnostic | 0.78 |
| Radiopharmaceuticals | 0.14 |
| Occupational | 0.01 |
| Miscellaneous | 0.05 |
| Subtotal | 1.06 |
| TOTAL | 1.86 |

a1 mSv equals 1 1000th Sv, or 0.1 rem.
bValues in parentheses indicate range over which average levels for different states
  vary with elevation.
cRange of variation (shown in parentheses) attributable largely to geographic differences in the content of potassium-40, radium, thorium, and uranium in the
  earth's crust.
                                                              (From BEIR, 1980)

for the U.S. population (Table 5-1).  Other effects, such as an increase in the incidence of cancer or genetic disease, may conceivably occur in response to any amount of radiation, varying only in frequency as a function of the dose. Thus, while early radiation sickness and mortality will be confined to those who are heavily irradiated, the risk of cancer and genetic disease may be increased in those who are exposed to only small amounts of fallout, hundreds or thousands of kilometers distant from ground zero.

The scientific bases for assessing radiation effects and for projecting the relative numbers of persons who may experience different types of effects as a result of nuclear detonations have been reviewed in detail elsewhere (Office of Technology Assessment, 1979; Coggle and Lindop, 1982: World Health Organization, 1983).   It is within the scope of this discussion merely to summarize the salient conclusions that have emerged from previous reviews as to how augmented radiation in the environment may affect human health.

## Short-term Effects (First 1-2 Months)

A dose of 2-10 gray (Gy), if absorbed within minutes or days, can kill sufficient numbers of germinative cells in the blood-forming tissues, skin, scalp, bone marrow, gastrointestinal tract, lung, and gonads to interfere with normal function in these organs.  The threshold dose required to cause clinical symptoms varies from organ to organ as can be seen on Table 5-2.  The frequency and severity of damage to the human body also depends on the conditions of irradiation, age at exposure, physiological status of exposed tissues, and other variables (Upton, 1968; Rubin and Casarett, 1968; UNSCEAR, 1982).   The unit commonly used for measuring or expressing the radiation dose in humans is the gray (Gy), Another commonly used unit is the sievert (Sv).

Injury of sufficient severity to cause early death from acute radiation sickness is thought to require a dose in excess of 2-3 Gy of whole-body radiation, with the probability of death reaching 100 percent in the range of 8-10 Gy if the dose is absorbed within a few days (see, for instance, Fig. 5-1).  With prolongation of the period of irradiation, adaptive reactions enable a progres-

Table 5-2

Estimated Threshold Doses of Acute Irradiation for
Clinical Evidence of Injury in Various Organs

| Organ | Effect | Dose (Gy) |
|-------|--------|-----------|
| Skin | Erythema (reddening) | 6-8 |
| Scalp | Loss of hair | 3-5 |
| Bone Marrow | Depression of blood count | 0.5-1 |
| Intestine | Ulceration | 8-10 |
| Testis | Depression of sperm count | 0.2 |
| Lymph Nodes | Atrophy | 0.5-1 |
| Lung | Pneumonitis | 6-8 |

(From Rubin and Casarett, 1968; UNSCEAR, 1982)

sively larger dose to be tolerated as shown in
Fig. 5-2. Thus, a total body exposure of 9 Gy
over 52 weeks would have the same probability of
lethality as a total exposure of 3-5 Gy for the
first week.

Although the dose-survival relationships de-
picted in Figs. 5-1 and 5-2 have been well characterized in experimental animals, they cannot be
defined precisely for human populations, owing to
the paucity of relevant data. Nevertheless, from
observations on atomic-bomb survivors, radiation
accident victims, and therapeutically irradiated
patients, the response can be delineated in broad
outlines (see Table 5-3 and Figs. 5-3a,b,c).

Table 5-3

================================================================

Symptoms and Clinical Signs of Radiation Sickness

Prodromal Manifestations

| Anorexia | Apathy | Fever |
| Nausea | Prostration | Respiratory Distress |
| Vomiting | Perspiration | Hyperexcitability |
| Diarrhea | Erythema | Ataxia |
| Fatigue | Conjunctivitis | |

Latent Period

No Symptoms

Main Illness

| Fever | Infection | Shock |
| Anorexia | Hemorrhage | Ataxia |
| Lassitude | Erythema | Agitation |
| Fatigue | Tanning | Disorientation |
| Weakness | Epilation | Convulsions |
| Weight Loss | Aspermia | Coma |
| Diarrhea | Ileus | |

(From Upton, 1969)

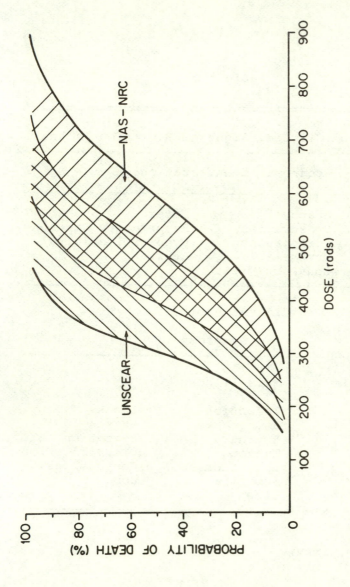

Fig. 5-1.  Probability of death after acute whole-body irradiation in man as a function of dose (modified from Langham et al., 1965). Overlapping range estimates are those of NAS-NRC (1960), UNSCEAR (1962), and Martin (1983) (intermediate, cross-hatched area).

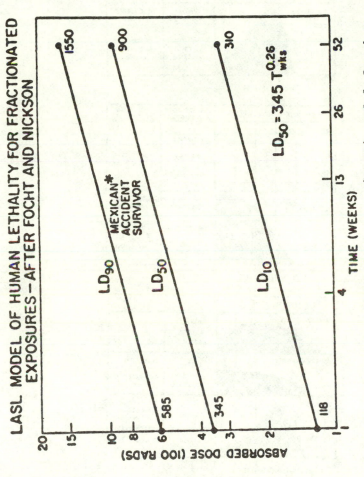

Fig. 5-2. The Los Alamos Scientific Laboratory (LASL) model for human lethality, computed from clinical total-body irradiation data of Focht and Nickson using the method of Strandqvist to determine the power function for duration of exposure in weeks (modified from Luchbaugh et al., 1982).

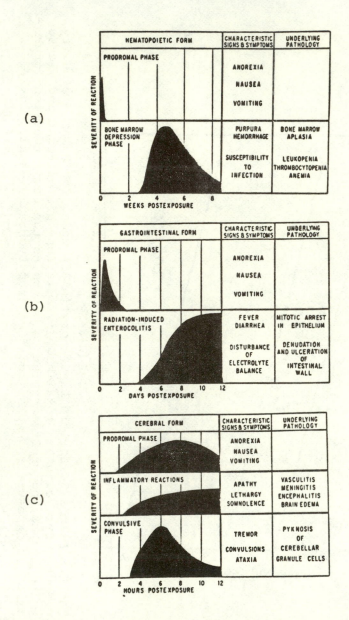

Figs. 5-3a,b,c. Salient features of the (a) hemo-
poietic (threshold, approximately 2 Gy), (b)
gastrointestinal (threshold, approximately
10 Gy), and (c) cerebral (threshold, approximately 50 Gy) forms of the acute radiation
syndrome in man (From Gerstner, 1958)

Table 5-4

Size of Area of Lethal Damage from Different
Types of Effects of Nuclear Bombs

| Type of Damage | Explosive Yield | | | | |
| | 1 kt | 10 kt | 100 kt (area in km$^2$) | 1 Mt | 10 Mt |
|---|---|---|---|---|---|
| Blast | 1.5 | 4.9 | 17.7 | 71 | 313 |
| Heat | 1.3 | 11.2 | 74.2 | 391 | 1583 |
| Radiation | 2.9 | 5.7 | 11.5 | 22 | 54 |

(From Barnaby and Rotblat, 1982)

The extent to which radiation injury may contribute to the early mortality caused by a nuclear
weapon will depend on the yield of the weapon, the
altitude at which it is detonated, and other factors (e.g., Office of Technology Assessment, 1979;
Coggle and Lindop, 1982; Duffield and von Hippel,
chapter 2). With weapons in the megaton range,
the area of lethal injury from blast and thermal
effects is estimated to equal or exceed that for
lethal injury from directly emitted ionizing radiation (Table 5-4). With large weapons, therefore,
exposure to radioactive fallout during the post-
attack period can be expected to constitute the
principal cause of early radiation mortality.

The distribution of the fallout from an atomic bomb will depend on the altitude at which the
bomb is exploded and on the weather conditions
prevailing at and following the time of explosion. With high-altitude bursts, much of the
fallout is carried into the stratosphere and dis-
persed globally. With surface bursts, on the
other hand, the distribution tends to be more localized. Although, as shown in Fig. 5-4, fallout
decays at a rate that can be predicted relatively

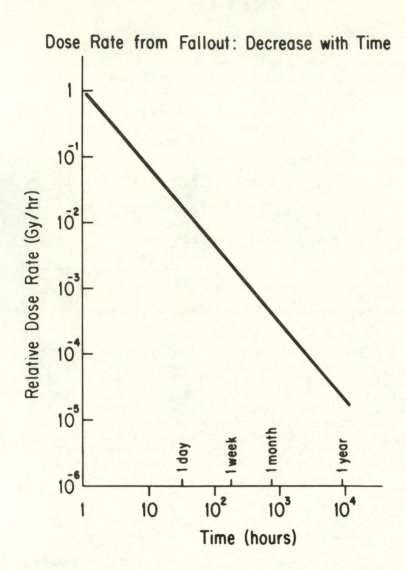

Fig. 5-4. Decrease with time in the dose rate from fallout.

(From Barnaby and Rotblat, 1982)

precisely, the distribution of radiation doses
that a population may receive from fallout in a
nuclear war will depend on many unpredictable
variables; e.g., the numbers, types, and yields of
weapons; the locations and altitudes at which they
are exploded, prevailing weather conditions, and
the extent to which the population at risk is able
to avoid or reduce radiation exposure by sheltering and other countermeasures (Machta, chapter 3).
Because of these variables, projected isodose
areas (e.g., Table 5-5, Fig. 5-5) provide only a
crude basis for estimating the radiation doses to
populations.

Table 5-5

Estimated Area Receiving
Given Accumulated Doses from Fallout

| Upper Limit of Accumulated Dose (rads) | Area ($km^2$) | |
|---|---|---|
| | 1-Mt Bomb | 10-Mt Bomb |
| 1,000 | 900 | 11,000 |
| 800 | 1,200 | 14,000 |
| 600 | 1,700 | 18,000 |
| 400 | 2,600 | 27,000 |
| 200 | 5,500 | 52,000 |
| 100 | 10,500 | 89,000 |
| 50 | 18.600 | 148,000 |
| 25 | 32,700 | 232,000 |
| 10 | 56,000 | 414,000 |

(From Barnaby and Rotblat, 1982)

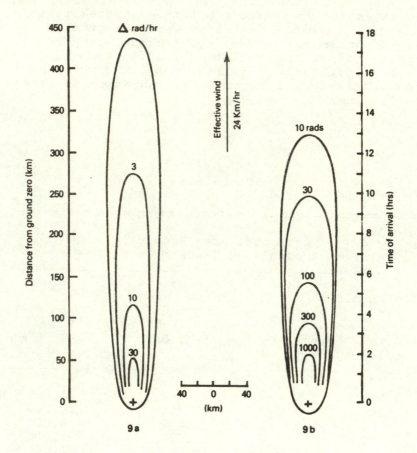

Fig. 5-5. Contours for fallout from a 2-Mt
bomb 18 hours after the explosion:
a) dose rates, and
b) total dose.
(From Barnaby and Rotblat, 1982)

For the above reasons, the short-term health effects of a nuclear war will depend heavily on the particular bomb scenario in question. Illustrative estimates of the numbers of casualties to be expected in different scenarios have been provided by the Office of Technology Assessment (Table 5-6). These indicate that a full-scale nuclear exchange would result in a holocaust of unprecendented proportions owing to the effects of radiation during the first two months combined with blast and thermal effects. As outlined in chapters 1 and 2, the range of possible scenarios is immense, and the effects expected from some of the more limited ones would be of a different magnitude than those expected from a major one.

## Middle-Term Effects (2 Months to 2 Years)

The extensive devastation resulting from a large-scale nuclear exchange would destroy much of the social infrastructure essential to normal shelter, heat, light, transportation, nutrition, sanitation, water supplies, public health, and medical care, with drastic impacts on health as shown in Table 5-7. Three consequences of a nuclear attack are described in detail in the report and appendices of the World Health Organization (1983). Under those conditions, and with millions of those surviving the initial lethal effects of the bombs left homeless, seriously injured and debilitated, infections and parasitic diseases would likely become rampant (Table 5-8; Fig. 5-6). The full extent of the resulting morbidity and mortality cannot be estimated with certainty.

Depending upon the particular combinations of detonation characteristics, some of the same processes would be at work under other scenarios. In any event, the deterioration of infrastructure could exacerbate the effects in the middle term.

## Long-Term Effects (2 + Years)

As noted above, the genetic and carcinogenic effects of radiation are generally postulated to have no threshold (UNSCEAR, 1977, 1982; BEIR, 1980). As a result, any exposure to radiation is expected to increase the frequency of cancer and genetic disease, roughly in proportion to the dose

Table 5-6

Estimates of Early Mortality from Various Types of Nuclear Weapons Attacks on the
U.S. or the USSR

| Scenario | Description | Main Causes of Civilian Damage | Immediate Deaths | Middle-term Effects |
|---|---|---|---|---|
| 1) 1-Mt air burst (s) | Attack on a single city, e.g., Detroit or Leningrad; 1 weapon or 10 small weapons. | Blast, fire, and loss of infra-structure; fallout where. | 200,000-2,000,000 | Many deaths from injuries; center of city difficult to rebuild. |
| 2) 80 1-Mt surface bursts | Attack on oil refineries; limited to 10 missiles. | Blast, fire, secon-dary fires, fallout. Extensive economic problems from loss of refined petroleum. | 1,000,000-5,000,000 | Many deaths from injuries; great economic hardship for some years; particular prob-lems for Soviet agriculture and for U.S. socio-economic organiza-tion. |

| | | | | |
|---|---|---|---|---|
| 3) 2100 1-Mt air and surface bursts | Counterforce attack; includes attack only on ICBM silos as a variant. | Some blast damage if bomber and missile submarine bases attacked. | 1,000,000–20,000,000 | Economic impact of deaths; possible large psychological impact. |
| 4) Comprehensive attack, air and surface bursts, up to 6500 Mt | Counterforce attack; includes attack only on ICBM silos as a variant. | Blast and fallout; subsequent economic disruption; possible lack of resources to support surviving population or economic recovery. Possible breakdown of social order. Possible incapacitating psychological trauma. | 20,000,000–160,000,000 | Enormous economic destruction and disruption. If immediate deaths are in low range, more tens of millions may die subsequently because economy unable to support them. Major question about whether economic viability can be restored—key variable may be those of political and economic organization. Unpredictable psychological effects. |

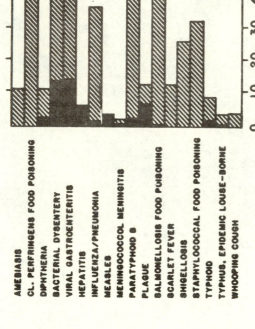

**% OF SURVIVORS**

AMEBIASIS
CL. PERFRINGENS FOOD POISONING
DIPHTHERIA
BACTERIAL DYSENTERY
VIRAL GASTROENTERITIS
HEPATITIS
INFLUENZA/PNEUMONIA
MEASLES
MENINGOCOCCOL MENINGITIS
PARATYPHOID B
PLAGUE
SALMONELLOSIS FOOD POISONING
SCARLET FEVER
SHIGELLOSIS
STAPHYLOCOCCAL FOOD POISONING
TYPHOID
TYPHUS, EPIDEMIC LOUSE-BORNE
WHOOPING COUGH

INCIDENCE
MORTALITY

Fig. 5-6. Estimated incidence of, and mortality from, acute epidemic disease among survivors in the U.S. population exposed to a large-scale nuclear attack. The composite figures show (in black) the anticipated mortality and (in the hatched areas) the incidence of various diseases. The figures assume no medical countermeasure and are based on the best available estimates from a variety of sources. The estimates are uncertain, however, owing to variation in the magnitude, timing, and locale of the attack. In a conflict of lessened intensity, in which medical resources could be exploited, mortality figures would be reduced correspondingly (from Abrams and von Kaenel, 1981).

Table 5-7

Various Medical Problems During the Attack and Post-Attack Periods

| Medical Problems* | Barrage Period First Hour | Shelter Period First Day | Shelter Period First 0-4 Wk | Survival Period (2 mos- 2 yrs) | Recovery Period (2+Yrs) Long-term Effects | Recovery Period (2+Yrs) Future Generations |
|---|---|---|---|---|---|---|
| Flash burns | + | - | - | - | - | - |
| Trauma and blast injury | + | - | - | - | - | - |
| Flame burns and smoke inhalation | + | + | - | - | - | - |
| Acute radiation | + | + | - | - | - | - |
| Fallout radiation | + | + | + | + | - | - |
| Suffocation and heat prostration | - | + | + | - | - | - |
| General lack of medical care | - | + | + | + | - | - |
| Dehydration | - | - | + | - | - | - |
| Communicable diseases | - | - | + | + | - | - |
| Exposure and hardship | - | - | + | + | - | - |
| Malnutrition | - | - | + | + | - | - |
| Cancer | - | - | - | - | + | - |
| Genetic damage | - | - | - | - | - | + |

*Listed in the approximate chronologic order in which they appear.

(From Abrams and von Kaenel, 1981)

Table 5-8

=================================================

Diseases Potentially Epidemic
During Post-Attack Period

Existing Epidemic Diseases of Low Incidence

Cholera
Malaria
Plague
Shigellosis
Smallpox
Typhoid fever
Typhus
Yellow Fever


Serious Existing Diseases

Diarrhea
Diphtheria
Hepatitis
Influenza
Meningitis
Pneumonia
Tuberculosis
Whooping Cough

Table 5-9

===========================================================

Estimated Cumulative Lifetime
Cancer Risks of Radiation

- - - - - - - - - - - - - - - - - - - - - - - - - - - - -

| Site of Cancer | Risk per 10,000 persons - Sv[a] | |
| | Fatal Cancers | Incident Cancers |
| --- | --- | --- |
| Breast (women only) | 50 | 50-200 |
| Thyroid | 10 | 20-150 |
| Lung | 25-50 | 25-100 |
| Bone Marrow (leukemia) | 15-40 | 20-60 |
| Brain | | |
| Stomach | | |
| Liver | 10-15 | 15-25 |
| Colon | | |
| Salivary glands | | |
| Bone | | |
| Esophagus | | |
| Urinary bladder | 2-5 | 5-10 |
| Pancreas | | |
| Lymphatic tissue | | |
| Skin | 1 | 15-20 |
| Total (both sexes) | 100-250 | 300-400 |

[a]The unit commonly used for expressing the collective dose to a population is the person Sv. The collective dose represents the product of the average dose person times the number of persons irradiated; i.e., a dose of 1 Sv delivered to each member of a population of 10,000 would correspond to a collective dose of 10,000 person-Sv.

- - - - - - - - - - - - - - - - - - - - - - - - - - - - -

(From National Academy of Sciences (1972, 1980), UNSCEAR (1977), and Jablon and Bailar (1980))

Table 5-10

Estimates of Genetic Detriment Attributable to Parental Irradiation

| Type of Genetic Detriment | Natural Incidence | Effects of 1 mSy Gonadal Dose[a] | |
|---|---|---|---|
| | | First Generation | per Generation at Equilibrium |
| Dominant traits + diseases | 10,000 | 0.1-1 | 5-100 |
| Chromosomal + recessive traits + diseases | 10,000 | <1 | <4 |
| Recognized abortions | | | |
| Aneuploidy + polyploidy | 35,000 | 1.1 | 1.1 |
| XO | 9,000 | 0.3 | 0.3 |
| Unbalanced rearrangements | 11,000 | 7.2 | 9.2 |
| Congenital anomalies | 15,000 | | |
| Anomalies expressed after birth | 10,000 | 0.1-10 | 1-100 |
| Constitutional + degenerative diseases | 15,000 | | |
| Total (rounded) | 115,000 | 10-30 | 16-200 |

[a]Per million offspring.

(Modified from reports of the National Academy of Sciences (1972, 1980) and UNSCEAR (1977), based on an assumed doubling dose of 0.1-25 Sv)

(Tables 5-9 and 5-10). The cancers resulting from a given dose do not occur immediately but appear after a latent period of up to 40 years or more, depending on the type of malignancy in question (UNSCEAR, 1977; BEIR, 1980). The genetic effects, similarly, do not all appear in offspring of the first generation but are distributed over many successive generations, depending on the type of effect in question (UNSCEAR, 1977; BEIR, 1980).

Although no definite increase in genetic disease has been demonstrable in the children of atomic-bomb survivors of Hiroshima and Nagasaki (Shull et al., 1981), and although the overall excess of cancer in such survivors amounts to an increase of only about 3 percent of the normal incidence (Kato and Shull, 1982), the numbers of cancers and genetic (inherited) abnormalities projected by the Office of Technology Assessment to result throughout the world from a full-scale nuclear war would compare in magnitude with the numbers of early deaths (Table 5-11). A similar relationship would apply to smaller size exchanges. Hence no assessment of the health effects of nuclear warfare would be complete without taking into account the long-term effects, as well as the short-term effects. For exchanges of lesser magnitude the effects of short-term radiation and of global fallout would be of similar quality but less extensive.

The World Health Organization report concluded that a one megaton explosion over the city of London could cause 1,800,000 dead and 1,700,000 injured if detonated at low altitude and 1,600,000 dead and 1,600,000 injured if detonated at high altitude. Its estimate of fatalities from a 10,000 megaton exchange was 1,150,000,000, with only slightly less injured (World Health Organization, 1983).

Whatever the number and circumstances of detonations, the types and processes of effects would be the same: direct radiation could be highly significant in the short-term, global fallout would be important in the long-term, and both would be exacerbated by middle-term social disorganization.

Table 5-11

Long-term Radiation Effects from a Comprehensive Nuclear Exchange
Between the U.S. and the USSR

1. Estimated effects of an attack on military and economic targets in the U.S.,
   consisting of 3,325 weapons with a total yield of 6,500 Mt, and a mixture of
   air bursts and surface bursts; (the ranges indicated represent variations in
   degree of fallout protection):

(A) Effects Inside the U.S.

   ● Somatic Effects
       Cancer deaths                                    1,000,000-5,500,000
       Thyroid cancers                                  1,000,000-2,000,000
       Thyroid nodules                                  1,500,000-2,500,000

   ● Genetic Effects
       Abortions due to chromosomal damage                150,000-6,000,000
       Other genetic effects                              400,000-9,000,000

(B) Effects Outside the U.S.[a]:

   ● Somatic Effects
       Cancer deaths                                      900,000-9,000,000
       Thyroid cancers                                    about 3,200,000
       Thyroid nodules                                    about 4,500,000

   ● Genetic Effects
       Abortions due to chromosomal damage                500,000-5,000,000
       Other genetic effects                            1,500,000-15,000,000

2. Estimated effects[b] of an attack on military and economic targets in the Soviet Union, consisting of 5,660 weapons with a total yield of 1,300 Mt and a mixture of air bursts and surface bursts; (the ranges indicated represent variations in degree of fallout protection):

- Somatic Effects
  - Cancer deaths                              1,200,000-9,300,000
  - Thyroid cancers                            about 5,500,000
  - Thyroid nodules                            7,700,000-8,400,000

- Genetic Effects
  - Abortions due to chromosomal damage        320,000-8,000,000
  - Other genetic effects                      1,000,000-12,500,000

[a]Most worldwide fallout would be in the Northern Hemisphere, and it would be concentrated between 30° and 60° N latitude.

[b]Includes worldwide totals, but effects are greater in the target country than elsewhere.

_____

(From Office of Technology Assessment, 1979)

## Conclusions

From the foregoing, it may be concluded that the health impacts of a full-scale thermonuclear war would surpass in magnitude those of any previous disaster known to mankind. Depending on the particular scenario envisaged, the numbers of victims dying within a few weeks from the effects of nuclear weapons, including those of bomb-produced radioactive fallout, could well be in the millions or tens of millions. For those who survived the initial post-attack period, the degree of devastation, disruption, and residual radioactivity in regions surrounding the target areas would seriously threaten continuing health and survival. Among the millions of homeless, injured, and seriously ill survivors, lack of adequate shelter, food, water supplies, sanitation, and medical care would lead to lingering disability and death from epidemics of many kinds. Moreover, for decades following the war, tens of millions of additional victims would suffer illness and death from radiation-induced cancer and genetic diseases, even among those exposed to fallout thousands of kilometers distant from the places of detonation.

## References

Abrams, H. L. and von Kaenel, W., Special report, 1981: Medical problems of survivors of nuclear war. Infection and the spread of communicable disease. New Eng. J. Med. 303, 1226-1232.

Barnaby, F. and J. Rotblat, 1982: The effects of nuclear weapons, in Nuclear War: The Aftermath. A Special Ambio Publication. Pergamon Press, New York, 15-35.

Coggle, J. E. and P. J. Lindop, 1982: Medical consequences as radiation following a global nuclear war, Ambio XI, 59-71.

Gerstner, H. B., 1958: Acute clinical effects of penetrating nuclear radiation, J. Am. Med. Assn., 168, 381-388.

Jablon, S. and J. Bailar, 1980: The contribution of ionizing radiation to cancer mortality in the United States, Prev. Med. 9, 219-226.

Kato, H. and W. J. Shull, 1982: Studies of the mortality of a-bomb survivors. 7. Mortality, 1950-1978: Part 1. Cancer Mortality, Rad Res., 90, 395-432.

Langham, W. H., P. M. Brooks, D. Grahn, D. A. Adams, F. E. Holly, H. J. Curtis, D. P. Campbell, T. C. Galbraith, L. V. Gibbons, R. L.. Kloster, S. W. Rudman, V. D. Spear, and C. H. Warneke, 1965: Radiation biology and space environmental parameters in manned spacecraft design and operations, Aerospace Med., 36, 1-55.

Lushbaugh, C. C., K. F. Hubner, S. A. Fry, and R. S. Ricks, 1982: Is precision of human radiation tolerance estimates sufficient for radiation emergency treatment? in The Control of Exposure of the Public to Ionizing Radiation in the Event of Accident or Attack. Proceedings of a Symposium by the National Council on Radiation Protection and Measurements, April 27-29, NCRP, Bethesda, 46-57.

Martin, J. H., 1983: Human survival--radiation exposure levels. J. Radiol. Protect., 3, 15-23.

National Academy of Sciences-National Research Council, 1960: The Biological Effects of Atomic Radiation. Summary Reports. National Academy of Sciences, Washington, D.C.

National Academy of Sciences Advisory Committee on the Biologial Effects of Ionizing Radiation (BEIR), 1980: The Effects on Populations of Exposure to Low Levels of Ionizing Radiation, National Academy of Sciences, Washington, D.C.

Office of Technology Assessment, 1979: The Effects of Nuclear War, Congress of the United States, Washington, D.C.

Rubin, P. and G. W. Casarett, 1968: Clinical Radiation Pathology, Volumes I and II. W. B. Saunders Co., Philadelphia.

Schull, W. J., M. Otake, and J. V. Neel, 1981: Genetic effects of the atomic bombs: A reappraisal, Science, 213, 1220-1227.

United Nations Scientific Committee on the Effects of Atomic Radiation (UNSCEAR), 1977: Report to the General Assembly, Official Records, 17th Session, suppl. No. 16. (A/5216), United Nations, New York.

United Nations Scientific Committee on the Effects of Atomic Radiation (UNSCEAR), 1977: Sources and Effects of Ionizing Radiation, Report to the General Assembly, with Annexes, United Nations, New York.

United Nations Scientific Committee on the Effects
    of Atomic Radiation (UNSCEAR), 1982:  Ion-
    izing Radiation:  Sources and Biological Ef-
    fects, Report to the General Assembly, with
    Annexes, United Nations, New York.
Upton, A. C., 1968:  Effects of radiation on man,
    Ann. Rev. Nucl. Sci., 18, 495-528.
Upton, A. C., 1969:  Radiation injury.  Effects.
    Principles and Perspectives, Univ. of Chicago
    Press, Chicago.
World Health Organization (S. Bergstrom et al.)
    1983:  Effects of a Nuclear War on Health and
    Health Services, Report of the International
    Committee of Experts in Medical Sciences and
    Public  Health,  WHO  Publication  A36.12,
    Geneva.

*George M. Woodwell*

# 6. The Long-Term Ecological Effects of Nuclear War: Twilight for the Species?

## Abstract

The potential long-term effects of a nuclear war, from 1,000 weapons of 0.1 Mt to the total arsenal of more than 12,000 Mt, include mobilization of sufficient dust and soot into the atmosphere to darken and cool the earth. Temperatures can be expected to drop to sub-freezing levels for several weeks or several months. The biotic effects of the climatic changes, plus the effects of high exposure to ionizing radiation, will lead to the biotic impoverishment of the earth that includes the destruction of agricultural potential, the loss of as much as 50 percent of the earth's species, and the loss of primary productivity. These changes will follow the direct effects of blast, heat, and radiation from the fireballs themselves, and will be extensive and severe enough to raise question as to whether Homo sapiens will survive as a species.

## Introduction

Nuclear bombs now in the hands of the world's governmental leaders contain enough energy to replace for a few minutes the solar flux impingent on the whole earth. The total, 10-20,000 Mt, is equivalent to between 2 and 4 tons of TNT for each one of us. It is 5-10,000 times as much as all the bombs dropped in World War II. We could have a thousand World War IIIs for an evening's entertainment. And those who survived could have another thousand at a Saturday matinee for a month.

123

In the face of such catastrophe is there purpose in a more detailed analysis? There is. Obviously, someone's analysis has put us all in this peril. Further analysis will be required to remove us from it. We cannot know too much; nor can we question such purposes intensively enough. Low as the chance of war may be, and it seems not low at all, the consequences are so profound that every opportunity should be used to examine them in detail in the hope that common sense will recover. The conclusions of the current re-examination are still emerging and are worth every citizen's attention.

No one knows the precise circumstances surrounding a nuclear exchange, whether it will be large or small, localized or general. There have been various attempts to define a range of possible or probable circumstances, as outlined in chapters 1 and 2, and to estimate the ecological consequences of each.

Because the magnitude, number, and distribution of detonations is hypothetical, the analysis of their effects is speculative. Nevertheless, there are certain ecological effects about which much is know. This paper outlines the range of possible consequences, indicates the major lines along which analyses are proceeding, summarizes the evidence as to the effects of ionizing radiation on ecosystems, and outlines potential biotic effects of the climatic changes now anticipated.

## Climatic Effects of a Hostile Exchange of Nuclear Weapons

The direct effects of blast, heat, fire, and ionizing radiation in a 10,000 megaton exchange of nuclear weapons could be expected to kill $1.1 \times 10^9$ people immediately and to leave another $1.0 \times 10^9$ injured (World Health Organization, 1983; Duffield and von Hipple, chapter 2). These effects would occur in the hours and days following the war; they would be unprecedented in the sordid, continuing history of human brutality. But they would be a mere beginning.

Recent appraisals of the long-term effects of a wide range of potential nuclear wars show that there would be sufficient mobilization of dust, soot, and smoke into the troposphere and, probably into the stratosphere, to darken the surface of the earth. The result would be a warming of the upper atmosphere and a cooling of the earth's surface (Crutzen and Birks, 1982; Turco et al., 1984; Aleksandrov and Stenchikov, 1983). The cooling would start within days of the war and, depending on the size of the war and the height and geographical distribution of the blasts, would lower the average surface temperature of the earth by 25° - 50° C, to as much as 25° C or more below freezing. These effects might reach into the Southern Hemisphere and could be expected to persist for weeks or months. Recovery to normal climatic regimes would require several years. The effects can be anticipated from virtually any exchange that involves as many as 1,000 of the world's 50,000 or more weapons.

The major changes would occur immediately in the Northern Hemisphere where most weapons would be detonated, but the cooling would probably extend quickly into the Southern Hemisphere as well, especially if weapons are detonated there as seems probable. The severity of the effects is difficult to exaggerate. The greatest changes in temperature would occur in the interior of continents. Coastal areas would be stormy, if warmer than the interior. The large amount of particulate material in the atmosphere would speed the precipitation of the radioactive debris onto the ground, thereby increasing the total radiation exposure at ground level to an average of as much as 50 roentgens (R).

These conditions could be anticipated:

1. A reduction of the intensity of solar radiation at the surface of the earth hemispherically, possibly globally, to 0.1 percent of normal.

2. Surface temperature lowered hemispherically, possibly globally, to -25° to -30° C for several days or several weeks; sub-freezing temperatures for 2-5 months, possibly longer.

3. Total radiation exposures on the surface of the earth that may average 50 R. Humans might expect an additional exposure from internal emitters of as much as 50 R. (The mean lethal exposure to humans under these conditions might be expected to be half or less the 450 R figure com-

125

monly used for those who have access to medical attention. This topic is discussed in detail by Upton in chapter 5).

4. Local radiation exposures of hundreds to thousands of R in segments of the fallout fields immediately downwind from the bomb blasts. These areas globally can be expected to cover areas measured in millions of square kilometers.

5. In the period during which the atmosphere was clearing, the surface of the earth would be bathed in ultraviolet radiation that would be 50 percent higher than normal due to particle destruction of the atmospheric ozone layer. High UV would persist for several years.

Such changes have far-reaching biotic consequences in addition to the direct effects of heat, blast, and radiation discussed above. Civilization with its normal services would be destroyed. The dark and cold ionizing radiation would be pervasive and unyielding. All surface fresh water would quickly freeze. Forage for cattle and other livestock would freeze and wither; livestock would die of starvation and cold. So would people. The effects of prolonged darkness and cold are not subtle, especially in combination with the loss of social and political services.

## Biotic Effects

Biotic effects would extend to the mortality of most if not all crop plants and plants in the natural communities of the temperate zones and the tropics. Damage would be least in the temperate zones if the war occurred early in winter, but in most of the scenarios analyzed by Turco et al. (1983) the darkness and cold would extend far enough into the normal spring and even summer to affect the hardier plants. Tropical forests are especially vulnerable to short periods of cold that need not be much below normal tropical temperatures.

Plants and animals are vulnerable not only to prolonged darkness and cold, but also to high intensities of ionizing radiation. Certain plants such as Pinus rigida, the pitch pine, have mean lethal exposures in the same general range as that of man and other mammals. Forests of the temperate zone are vulnerable to severe damage from fallout exposures of 500 to 1,000 R or above, well

within the range of exposures in the areas downwind of bomb bursts (Woodwell, 1965, 1982). A
crude appraisal of the area affected by radiation
exposures of 1,000 R or more can be made on the
basis of the assumption that half the bursts affect forested areas and that a 1 Mt burst would
produce total fallout exposures in excess of 1,000
roentgens in a field over 500 $km^2$. Under these
circumstances a war of 5,700 Mt, such as that assumed in Ambio, would affect $1.4 \times 10^6$ $km^2$ or 3
percent of the forested area of the earth. To the
extent that the bursts are the same in total energy, but distributed among smaller warheads (the
mean warhead in the Ambio war was 400 kt), the assumption used here is an underestimation. The uncertainty in great enough that further detailed
elaboration is inappropriate.

Nonetheless, considerable experience is
available to define the patterns of changes in the
structure of natural communities produced by disturbances such as the anticipated climatic changes
and exposure to ionizing radiation as well as
other toxic insults. The patterns are those of
biotic impoverishment. The most detailed experience comes from an experiment with ionizing radiation, but the results have general application
(Woodwell,1970).

The experience has been with the systematic
exposure of an oak-pine forest in central Long
Island to chronic gamma radiation beginning in
1961 (Woodwell, 1970). Exposures ranges from more
than 1000 R/day within a few meters of a 9,500 Ci
Cs-137 source, to about 1 R/day at 125 m, and to
lower levels at greater distance.

The effects were spectacular and in-
structive. The forest was dissected layer by
layer as well as species by species. The pines,
Pinus rigida, were the most vulnerable of all species, but all the trees were more vulnerable than
the shrubs. Tall shrubs were more sensitive than
low-growing shrubs and the woody plants were more
sensitive than herbaceous plants. In the zones
where no higher plants survived, certain species
of lichens and mosses lived on. In herbs, mosses,
lichens, and shrubs, the most resistant were the
short-statured, ground-hugging species, the annu-
als, and the small-bodied with high reproductive
potential. The larger, longer-lived, and slower

127

to reproduce, were vulnerable. The mechanisms that underlie these results have been explored and there appears to be cytological and therefore genetic basis for some of the response (Woodwell, 1967).

Various reviews of other types of disturbances confirm the pattern as a general response to disturbance, one that can be applied to the effects of chronic mechanical disturbance, fire, toxic substances, and acid rain. It can also be applied to the varied insults of nuclear war: prolonged darkness, a sudden change in temperature, exposure to ionizing radiation, and, after the clearing of the atmosphere, high exposure to ultraviolet radiation.

The biotic effects are known. They are the classical changes of biotic impoverishment: extinction of species, destruction of forests, reduced primary production, and widespread mortality of higher plants, mammals, birds, and fish. Population explosions would occur among small-bodied, rapidly producing species of plants and animals, including the weeds of garden and roadside; the insect pests of house, garden, and forest; the rodent pests of house and field; the hardy, ubiquitous birds, fish, and mammals, and plants of polluted or otherwise chronically disturbed sites. These are the species that compete with man. They are not sources of sustenance, or even of comfort, nor are they effective in nature in providing the normal services in stabilizing landscapes, controlling of flows water, or in providing the myriad other services we expect of natural ecosystems in the normal course.

The Ambio scenario is partial, despite its comprehensiveness. The effects discussed are certain for the Northern Hemisphere, they are possible as well for the Southern. Human survival seems paramount. Without it other issues become academic.

This analysis emphasizes the longer-term ecological effects, which, on the basis of the most recent considerations, now appear to be fully as threatening as the immediate effects of blast, heat, and radiation. Beyond what has been covered in previous chapters, several conclusions about longer-term effects of any exchange deserve attention:

1. Assured effects (Office of Technology Assessment, 1979) calculated for military purposes underestimate actual damage, especially in the longer run of weeks, months, and years. Long-term ecological effects generally have been ignored in military estimates; as well as mortality due to fires, the destruction of crops, and exposure to internal emitters. The effects of the disruption of transportation and communication have also been ignored.

2. "Small" or "limited" nuclear exchanges, if any exchange can be so controlled, can be expected to have profound immediate and long-term ecological consequences not greatly different in effects on man from those of the larger exchanges that appear more probable.

3. There would be a significant mobilization or radioactivity into the atmosphere. Each bomb can be expected to produce a fallout field of hundreds to thousands of square miles. Radiation exposures will exceed the 250-500 R mean lethal exposure for man and approach exposures lethal for many higher plants.

4. Fallout radiation would destroy forests and other vegetation over extensive areas. Fires set at the time of the exchange would smolder over weeks and burn vegetation damaged by radiation or climatic changes. This type of widespread destruction of biotic resources fundamental to maintenance of the biosphere would add a further burden on any survivor of the immediate effects of the war.

5. The principles of biotic impoverishment would apply to a post-war world, which would be without forests, large mammals, or the stabilizing influences of a rich biota. It would be a world plagued by outbreaks of the small-bodied rapidly reproducing species commonly identified as pests.

In such uncertain circumstances as those that must exist following a nuclear war there is clearly great difficulty in identifying what issues are most important.

Human survival is surely in question, despite the vigor, imagination, and perseverance of Homo sapiens. Protection of those who survive the immediate effects of blast, heat, and radiation from weeks of darkness, cold, and continued high radiation is difficult to envision or to prepare. To the loss of social services, energy, and the benefits of technology must be added the further losses of nearly all crops and the normal supply of food, fiber, and services that biotic resources provide in managing the environment. Forests, killed by frost and radiation, can be expected to burn. Fires will rage for weeks, possibly months, adding soot to the atmosphere, prolonging the darkness and cold. People, reduced to small groups, deprived of their common technologies and sources of food, attempting to live on a frozen, dark, radioactive and stormy landscape without power or machines will be challenged suddenly to return to a stone age economy. If by some chance, that might be considered malevolent, people survive into the period of clearing of air and warming, they will be bathed in ultraviolet radiation at intensities 50 percent higher than normal, enough to burn, cause cancer and to effect a further increment of biotic impoverishment. In such circumstances it is difficult to envision that survival rates will be high. If a quarter of the global population succumbs directly to the immediate effects of the war, the destruction of resources caused by the change in climate would be sufficiently thorough to assume that between half and all the remainder would die in the next few weeks. The potential effects are almost beyond imagination. They clearly extend to the possibility, perhaps the certainty, of human extinction. And the Ambio war is, after all, a mere third of the war we might have.

## References

Aleksandrov, V. V., and G. L. Stenchikov, 1983: On the Modelling of the Climatic Consequences of Nuclear War. The Computing Center of the Academy of Sciences of the USSR, Moscow.
Ambio, 1983: Nuclear War: The Aftermath. A Special Ambio Publication. Royal Swedish Academy of Sciences, Pergamon Press, Oxford.

Crutzen, P. J., and J. W. Birks, 1982: The atmosphere after a nuclear war: twilight at noon, Ambio, XI, 114-125.

Office of Technology Assessment, 1979: The Effects of Nuclear War. Office of Technology Assessment, U. S. Congress, Washington, D.C.

Turco, R. P., O. B. Toon, T. P. Ackerman, J. B. Pollack, C. Sagan, 1983: Nuclear winter: global consequences of multiple nuclear explosions, Science, 222, 1283-1292.

Woodwell, G. M., ed., 1965: Ecological Effects of Nuclear War. BNL 917(C-43), Brookhaven National Laboratory, Upton, N. Y.

Woodwell, G. M., 1970: Effects of pollution on the structure and physiology of ecosystems, Science, 168, 429-33.

Woodwell, G. M., 1967: Radiation and the patterns of nature, Science, 156, 461-470.

Woodwell, G. M., 1982: The biotic effects of ionizing radiation, Ambio, XI, 143-148.

World Health Organization, 1983: Effects of Nuclear War on Health and Health Services, Report of the International Committee of Experts.

*Julius London, Gilbert F. White*

# 7. Current Unresolved Problems in the Evaluation of Environmental Effects of Nuclear War

## Abstract

Some uncertainties involving predictable and unpredictable environmental consequences of a large scale global nuclear exchange are identified and suggestions are made of specific topics where further studies should and could be pursued to narrow these uncertainties.

## Introduction

As a result of studies after the Hiroshima and Nagasaki explosions, the various bomb tests, by the U.S., USSR, and China, and laboratory and field experiments, many of the consequences of nuclear bomb explosions, particularly short-term local consequences, are reasonably well known. These experiences, however, all involved single detonations or experiments. Because of synergistic effects, and the fact that there has been no experience with global scale of multiple bursts, there is some uncertainty related to different aspects of longer-term local and global effects following a nuclear exchange. Many of the effects described in chapters 2-6 are subject to questions as to the validity of the basic data and the assumed physical and biological processes. These effects may be grossly overestimated. On the other hand, they may be severely underestimated. This latter case would, of course, have much more serious consequences. Uncertainties in either direction need to be recognized in order to avoid

133

discrediting estimates of the whole range of expected environmental effects.

An example of underestimating possible atmospheric effects following multiple bomb bursts over
a large area in a relatively short period of time
is the earlier suggestion, based on observation of
the lack of a strong climate response to large
volcanic explosions, that dust and smoke clouds
resulting from fires set off by nuclear explosions
would have minimal climate effects (e.g., National
Academy of Sciences, 1975). However, observations
from nuclear weapons tests show that bomb produced
dust is much more efficient in shielding the earth
from solar radiation than aerosols resulting from
even major volcanic eruptions. In addition, volcanic blasts are single events and the fallout
pattern from such blasts is not as extensive as
bomb explosions. Until the study of Crutzen and
Birks (1982) there had been no systematic analysis
of possible significant disturbances to the atmosphere as a result of smoke and soot from large and
widespread fires. Current atmospheric model experiments now indicate that there is a strong
likelihood that such smoke and dust clouds probably would produce severe climate changes.

There is also the haunting possibility of
other significant direct and indirect effects of a
global nuclear exchange that are as yet unidenti-
fied but cannot be excluded from concern, since
all too often our awareness of possible environmental effects of nuclear explosion has come from
'erratic and accidental discoveries'. This represents an inherent uncertainty in trying to evalu-
ate the full consequences of the long-term environmental effects. The problem of long-term
risk assessment in the face of estimated and as
yet unknown uncertainties associated with the effects of nuclear war arises because of the trade-
off between the probability of occurrence and the
likely severity of these effects. An excellent
analysis of this problem has recently been presented by Kennedy (Ehrlich et al., 1984).

The uncertainties associated with different
estimates of environmental nuclear war effects involve, among other things:
   a)   uncertainties in how and where such a war
        might be conducted, i.e., the so-called
        nuclear war scenarios;

b)  what is known from previous single nucle-
    ar bomb explosions;
c)  how valid are the time and areal extent
    extrapolations from these experiences;
d)  how valid are the results from models for
    which, fortunately, there is no previous
    experience; and
e)  what possible additional important fac-
    tors need to be explored.

Relatively little can be done about the first
item except to describe the full set of likely
scenarios with some emphasis on those that would
produce the more damaging effects. As outlined in
chapter 1, the consequences of a nuclear exchange
depend strongly on the:
>       number of warheads used;
>       mix of tactical and strategic weapons;
>       mix of equivalent energy yields of the
        weapons used;
>       mix of surface and upper air bursts;
>       dominant geographic locations of the
        attacks;
>       season during which the attacks take
        place; and
>       dominant weather pattern at the time of
        and following the attacks.

It is not possible to specify in advance the
conditions under which such a war might be
fought.  Indeed we have learned from past conflicts that there is no way that we can predict
with any reasonable certainty how a nuclear war,
once started, would develop. Although any of the
likely scenarios being used as input data for current analyses indicate devastating environmental
effects, these effects would be modified somewhat
depending on details of the scenario variables.
It would be desirable to conduct additional analyses to test the sensitivity of the model results
to the different scenarios and input assumptions.

The results of studies of local short-term
effects from single bomb detonations have been
quite well summarized (see, Glasstone and Dolan,
1977; Duffield and von Hipple, chapter 2).  These
effects are closely tied to the yield, height, and
location of the bomb burst.  As discussed in
chapter 1, they involve phenomena caused by the

a)  bomb blast such as surface cratering,
    disturbances to the local terrain and the
    severe blast structural damage resulting
    from the overpressure shock wave emanat-
    ing from the point of detonation. There
    is, however, insufficient information of
    surface disruption that might be caused
    over irregular terrain by high energy low
    altitude explosions;

b)  thermal radiation at temperatures of a
    few thousand degrees in the bomb cloud
    causing immediate flash burns to humans
    and animals, and ignition of combustible
    material in the vicinity of the bomb ex-
    plosion;

c)  ionizing (nuclear) radiation predominant-
    ly in the form of neutrons and gamma-rays
    immediately after the bomb detonation and
    subsequently as radioactive substances
    subject to local and extended fallout.
    The fallout is strongly dependent on
    atmospheric conditions including winds at
    all levels, the thermal stability of the
    atmosphere, and the rainfall pattern.
    These are important for prediction of the
    dispersal of the radioactive bomb debris
    but cannot be specified in advance. In-
    formation is available on how the fallout
    material would be transported under ob-
    served meteorological conditions (see,
    for instance, Machta, chapter 3; Kurada,
    et al., 1965).

Uncertainty arises in extrapolation of these
results to perturbed conditions. Some studies,
based on actual tests, have attempted to estimate
the insult to the ozone layer that would result
from single bomb explosions (see, for instance,
Foley and Ruderman, 1973; Johnston et al., 1973).
However, simple linear extrapolation from these
results have proven to be inadequate (see, Chang
and Wuebbles, chapter 4).

The most serious problem in extending the results of single bomb explosions to long-term effects involves the quantification of eventual fatalities and physiological damage including genetic disorders.

## Uncertainties in Model Results

It most certainly will not be possible to
directly verify the predicted environmental conse-

quences of a nuclear war. These consequences are catastrophic and it is essential that questions of the validity of the models and the bases for the model results be critically examined. Their resolution,however, would probably only quantitatively modify or fine tune the predicted sequelae.

The major problems that arise from the different model results deal with:

a)  the effects of smoke and dust clouds following the numerous bomb detonations,
b)  atmospheric models that predict, on the basis of physical, chemical and dynamic interactions, the subsequent climate and ocean-atmospheric circulation system, and
c)  ecological and human health responses to these changes, and to widespread fallout of radioactive substances.

The amount of energy released in a nuclear exchange involving a total of 5,000 Mt equivalent yield is equal to only about 2 minutes of solar radiation received by the entire earth and is less that $10^{-7}$ of the average kinetic energy of the global wind system. It is unlikely therefore that even such massive explosions would directly and significantly disrupt the basic global weather pattern. Parts of the atmospheric circulation, however, frequently border on a state of instability, and relatively small changes in the distribution of energy input to the atmosphere could often cause the outbreak of violent storms such as cyclones, hurricanes, and tornadoes. Also, a relatively small decrease in the average surface temperature over the earth, if it lasts for some years, could very well initiate an unstable growth of glaciers extending from polar regions (e.g., Budyko, 1974). Thus, large scale nuclear detonations could indirectly trigger important changes in the surface atmospheric thermal structure and wind patterns if such bombs would be responsible for variations in the vertical and horizontal distribution of solar energy absorbed in the atmosphere.

The model results cited in chapters 1 and 6 (e.g., Crutzen and Birks, 1982; Turco et al., 1983) have indicated that extended clouds of dust, smoke, and soot caused by the bomb explosions directly, and by bomb produced conflagrations, could significantly alter this distribution so that for some weeks or months most of the incoming solar radiation would be absorbed in the upper troposphere rather than be transmitted to the earth's surface. The magnitude of the resulting atmospheric changes would depend on how much smoke and dust is injected into the atmosphere, the height to which the aerosol particles are lifted, and their physical and chemical characteristics. For smoke generated by fires, it is important to estimate quantitatively how the fires would spread and how long they would continue to burn. Because such events could have devastating environmental effects, physical processes involved in the atmospheric models need to be carefully evaluated and areas of insufficient information need to be identified.

### Some Uncertainties Involving the Smoke and Dust Cloud

There are four major sources of nuclear bomb produced smoke and dust, each of which gives rise to differences in cloud particle characteristics. These sources are:

a) dust resulting from vaporization and vertical uplift of surface material,
b) fires affecting forests, crops, and grassland,
c) fires involving urban and industrial areas, and
d) fires involving fuel reservoirs and natural gas/oil lines.

Although some information is available on dust clouds resulting from past bomb tests, very little is known of the dynamics of fire plumes or of the physical and chemical properties (i.e., size and composition) of the aerosol residues from fires, particularly its elemental carbon content (Crutzen and Galbally, 1984). Most important for the calculation of the cloud opacity is the lack of adequate data on the spectral distribution in the visible and infrared of the different cloud particles. The residence time of the smoke and dust particles in the atmosphere would depend on the height and size distributions of the aerosols. Both are subject to variation. Better quantitative information on these variations than is presently available is required if uncertainty as to the character of the initial plumes is to be reduced.

What happens to the airborne particles after injection into the atmosphere as a result of the bomb detonation and extensive fires? Most of the large particulates can settle out as dry deposition in a matter of a few days. Smaller particles, however, typically on the order of 0.1 μm to a few μm have residence times of weeks to months depending on the level to which they are lifted. These particles grow slowly with time as a result of coagulation and they act as cloud condensation nuclei (CCN). Although both of these processes are generally understood (see, for instance, Prupacher and Klett, 1978), application to smoke particles is not well documented and requires additional study.

The particles are removed from the atmosphere mostly by precipitation scavenging (wet deposition). A large increase in the CCN would also increase the number of small cloud droplets and sharply reduce the rate of precipitation. As a result, the aerosol removal rate would also be reduced and the atmospheric residence time of the smoke and dust cloud particles would be increased. This would have two very important consequences. The atmospheric effects of the smoke and dust particles would persist for a protracted period of time and, as a result, the airborne aerosols and radioactive substances would be spread over a much larger area, extending the deleterious climate and health effects far beyond the bomb explosion regions. However, it is normally assumed, because of the predicted thermal stability of the upper troposphere, that the smoke cloud will spread uniformly. But this needs to be the result of, rather than input to, the model calculations. In addition, the aerosol growth rate and the efficiency of the precipitation scavenging process are not well enough known, and definitive studies are urgently needed to resolve this important problem.

The predicted depletion of solar radiation and subsequent precipitous cooling of Northern Hemisphere continental areas is based, in part, on the optical properties of the smoke and dust particles assumed in the various models. The absorption and scattering characteristics of these aerosols are wavelength and particle size dependent. Also, for particles that are not strongly absorbing in the visible, downward scattering of solar radiation could reduce the cooling effect at the surface and needs to be considered in the models. Much of this information has recently become available and should be included in future calculations of atmospheric effects.

As a result of the bomb explosions and intense fires there would also probably be an increase in trace gases in the lower troposphere, which if persistent, could eventually produce a small greenhouse warming of the surface. Although this effect is likely to be small, it needs to be carefully evaluated.

## Problems Involving Atmospheric Models

The earth's atmosphere is a large complex interactive physical/chemical/hydrodynamic three dimensional system, and there are no known methods to predict its future state with absolute certainty. At the same time, the atmosphere has tremendous inertia, and it is possible to derive qualitative and even semi-quantitative information of how it would respond to a severe insult to the system.

The simplest model that can be used to provide a first order realistic picture of meteorological effects of the type discussed in this chapter is a time-dependent 1-D radiative-convecting model (RCM). (These models are discussed, for instance, by Ramanathan and Coakley, 1978.) RCMs have been used with input assumptions of the distribution and physical/optical characteristics of smoke and dust injected into the atmosphere as a result of bomb detonations and extensive fires produced initially by the high temperatures in the bomb cloud. The 1-D RCMs have dramatically shown the devastating changes at the earth's surface that are likely to occur as a result of nuclear war (e.g., Turco et al., 1983). These models, however, need to be improved. For example, more complete radiative transfer calculations should be included in the models, particularly for the lower troposphere where the infrared effects of increased traces gases could be important. More realistic treatment of the oversimplified lower boundary conditions and of the vertical transport of heat and aerosols in the model are also required. It is possible that the predicted surface effects, if these persisted for some time, could result in significant large scale albedo changes. The albedo/climate feedback accompanying these changes could have serious consequences and should be modeled.

The change in the vertical temperature distribution predicted by the 1-D model would represent a perturbation to the atmospheric system. The effects of this perturbation cannot be easily accounted for by this model. It is not able to produce realistic horizontal temperature differences, particularly in boundary areas between oceans and continents, nor can the model adequately portray components of the hydrological cycle. The horizontal transport and fallout of smoke, dust, and radioactive debris can also not be determined by these models. Refinement of the surface temperature effects and prediction of the latitudinal and interhemispheric transport of the airborne material require that a 2-D or 3-D general circulation model be employed. At the same time it is important to recognize that preliminary computation using simplified 2-D and 3-D general circulation models (e.g., MacCracken, 1983; Aleksandrov and Stenchikov, 1983; Covey et al., 1984) have verified the principal results of the 1-D models.

One of the major problems associated with 1-D atmospheric models is their inability to properly incorporate the different feedback processes that occur when the atmosphere is significantly disturbed. For instance, the large predicted heating in the upper atmosphere and the cooling at the surface would, according to the different model calculations, vary geographically and these variations would strongly modify the aerosol transport. But the heating and cooling distributions, in turn, are determined by the distribution of the aerosols. In a similar way, the hydrological cycle modifies and is modified by the 3-D general circulation pattern. Of course, variations in aerosol transport and the hydrological cycle both seriously affect the fallout pattern over the globe. Many improvements have recently been made in the 3-D climate models (see, for instance, Williamson, 1983) but no fully interactive dynamic model, including a complete hydrological cycle and ocean coupling, is yet available. Improved 1-D models need to be used to test the sensitivity of the various predicted results to uncertainties in the prescribed input variables. Ultimately, however, 3-D models must be used for better quantitative prediction of intermediate to long-term fallout patterns and trans-hemispheric consequences, since the fallout distribution strongly depends on the perturbed atmospheric circulation and the rainfall scavenging that varies with the vertical thermal stability and dominant global synoptic weather patterns.

The results of various atmospheric model calculations have also shown that high yield nuclear weapons exploded according to a normally assumed pattern would result in a total column decrease of ozone. The computed reduction depends somewhat on the weapons scenario and is about 50-60 percent when either 1-D (Chang and Wuebbles, chapter 4) or 2-D (Crutzen and Birks, 1982) models are used. In either case, the ozone decrease would result in a significant increase in the biologically damaging ultraviolet radiation received at the ground (see, for instance, Pyle and Derwent, 1980; Zandecki and Gerstl, 1982). However, atmospheric disturbances in the upper troposphere and lower stratosphere following a series of nuclear blasts would alter the latitudinal spread of stratospheric nitrogen oxides and thus might change the pattern of total ozone reduction. A better approximation to the global distribution of likely ozone reduction therefore needs to be derived from a 3-D radiative/photochemical/dynamic interactive model that includes tropospheric-stratospheric coupling. In addition, it is necessary to include the time variations of overhead aerosols for realistic calculations of the subsequent increase in the harmful UV-B radiation.

## Fallout Effects on the Fresh Water System

Radionuclides enter the biosystem directly as deposition on human, animal, and vegetal surfaces through inhalation from atmospheric contamination, and indirectly, by ingestion through the fresh water system and vegetation uptake from contaminated soils. The fresh water contamination depends strongly on the local hydrological cycle: the surface water regimen, storage in snow and ice, and the aquifers.

It is necessary that estimates be made of the changes that would occur in the character of the

142

vadose zone. That is, what would be the effect of surface and near surface bomb explosions on the geological structure and fluid dynamic properties of the subsoil system? Since different radio-nuclides are transported through the soil at different rates it is also important that local studies be conducted to determine the radionuclide flow through the unsaturated zone as well as the local aquifers.

Most of the radionuclide depositions on the surface is from rain and snow scavenging. A portion of these nuclides become concentrated in surface water reservoir systems whose primary supply comes from large catch basins and melt from extended snow pack areas. Some preliminary studies have indicated that these reservoirs can produce long-term delayed significant contamination of the downstream water (Wetzel, 1982). These studies need to be extended to different local conditions and results need to be quantitatively documented.

## Uncertainties Involving Biospheric Effects

Uncertainties in the biospheric response to massive nuclear explosions are inherent in the different uncertainties of model predictions of drastic depletion of solar visible and near infrared radiation, and the subsequent sudden lowering of the surface temperature over continental regions. In addition, neither the model-derived large scale transport of smoke, dust, and radioactive debris, nor the fallout pattern of the radioactive substances is sufficiently well known to be estimated with the necessary precision. But even if these could be predicted relatively accurately from the atmospheric models, other questions would still need to be answered. For instance: How do large different species in the ecosystem respond to short-term significant surface temperature variations? or to sharply decreased loss of sunlight over periods of a few weeks to a few months? How drastically would this response result in significantly reduced food production? How are these effects dependent on the onset of these disturbances during different phases of the growing cycle? or to enhanced UV-B radiation over an extended period as a result of the predicted ozone decrease?

Although, because of the high heat capacity of water, surface temperature changes over the

oceans are predicted to be quite small, on the
order of a few degrees at most, more quantitative
information is needed concerning the effect of the
depletion of sunlight on marine photobiotic systems.

Nuclear radiation damage from direct neutron
and gamma-ray radiation immediately following bomb
bursts is fairly well known, but intermediate and
hemispheric/global long-term effects on the biosphere are only qualitatively known and much more
research on this problem is needed. Assuming the
atmospheric transport of various radioisotopes and
their fallout patterns are reasonably well understood, we are still left with the complex exercise
of charting the continued pathway of these radioisotopes through the surface and ground water systems, the soil environment, and through incorpor-
ation into the food chain. To what extent is the
problem made more difficult if most of the fallout
occurs during the growing season? or harvest time?

Additional unresolved questions which require
further study are:
1)  How much direct damage is likely to af-
    fect the biosystem as a result of burning
    of forests, grass, and croplands?
2)  What is the probable degree of insult to
    the biosphere as a result of increased
    toxicity from low level air pollution
    following large urban/industrial fires?
3)  How would the biosphere respond to dras-
    tic perturbations to the rainfall distri-
    bution should these changes occur?

There is little hard evidence, at present, to
assess the extent of radiation damage to living
plants and animals from delayed fallout over large
areas. Some specific resultant mutations in the
ecosystem are predictable so that it can be infer-
red that the surviving population might have to
quickly accommodate itself to new biological
strains. There are strong suggestions that some
radiation damage could cause irreversible adverse
effects on the ecosystem. It is simply not known
how long it would be before food production could
be revived and stabilized to sustain the surviving
population.

These factors could very well have interrelated effects on the biosphere that would syner-

gistically increase the injury to the entire system. But there is little experience available to quantify these combined effects.

## Uncertainties Related to Civilian Casualties

Estimates of the total number of casualties, both deaths and injuries, must of necessity be soft since these casualties depend so strongly on unpredictable details of a nuclear bomb exchange. These details involving, among other things, scenario particulars as discussed earlier in this chapter, are most pertinent in estimating the immediate casualties. However, as the time and space scales increase, the specifics of the bombing scenarios become somewhat less important and the casualty level would be increased as a result of interrelated cumulative effects as discussed below. The total casualty estimates are so high, of the order of half the world's population (World Health Organization, 1983), that possible uncertainties of 50 percent or so have little meaning.

As discussed by Upton (see chapter 5), much is known about sickness and disease associated with exposure to nuclear radiation, but it is difficult to extrapolate from the Hiroshima and Nagasaki experiences the very long-term cancer increases to be expected. Also, there is sufficient data available from laboratory experiments with animals (see, for instance, Coggle and Lindop, 1982; World Health Organization, 1983) to suggest that genetic effects following extensive population exposure to nuclear radiation is a matter of urgent concern. Although there is no statistically significant evidence of genetic damage among the offspring born to exposed Hiroshima and Nagasaki parents (Schull et al., 1981), the possible long delay between exposure and consequent appearance of genetic effects coupled with the widespread fallout that would affect the surviving population indicates the need for a high priority for continued research on nuclear radiation induced genetic disturbances in humans.

The high casualty levels discussed here would certainly lead to a confused and paralyzed social environment without taking account of destruction of infrastructure and community facilities. However, there is almost a complete lack of information on which to base estimates concerning how the necessary support functions could be developed to sustain and rebuild the remnant society (Katz, 1982). This would involve provisions for adequate food and shelter, water, medical personnel and facilities, control of sanitation facilities, pest and pathogen control, fire and civil police control systems, and general maintainence of social order. Although the direct EMP effects on different electric circuit systems are known, there is also only limited experience for estimating the resultant social and psychological impact of a severe sudden breakdown of telephone, radio, and satellite communications networks.

There is no solid basis for judging the likely social responses to the disruption that might ensue from a nuclear holocaust. Much is known about the immediate emergency response and long-term recovery and reconstruction following natural disasters such as the Bengal tropical cyclone of 1970 or the Tangsham earthquake of 1976 (Burton et al., 1978). However, in those instances, as with the Sahalian drought of the 1960s or with territories devastated during World War II, the regions of suffering were in communication with adjoining or distant areas remaining relatively undisturbed. Thus, communications systems, emergency air, and reconstruction could be mounted from the outside. With the exception of localities strewn with land mines or herbicides, most of those areas retained their basic life supporting capacity in air, soil, water, and plants. Similarly, the Hiroshima and Nagasaki bomb explosions disrupted all local medical and civil facilities so that all support services had to come from outside. The lands affected by nuclear destruction would be impaired and it is not known how severe would be the limitations to these 'outside' resources.

It also should be noted that while there are instances of major evacuations of populations carried out effectively in anticipation of disaster, as along hurricane coasts, not all such exercises have been successful. Neither have they been executed over large regions or under the threat of the massive destruction expected from nuclear detonations.

In estimating social consequences from a single nuclear explosion the evidence from comparable localized technological and natural disasters

probably is as hard or harder than the evidence
for estimating physical and biological consequences.  Relatively accurate judgments can be
made as to evacuation operations and the manner in
which aid and rehabitation may be provided.  When
more extensive destruction over large areas, or
simultaneously in many locations, is contemplated,
the opposite probably is the case:  estimates of
social response must be highly speculative at
best.

## Synergies

Although it has been noted at many points in
the preceding pages, we emphasize the extent to
which synergistic relationships play a role in
shaping the consequences examined.  They are
numerous and not well understood.

At the local scale, for example, there have
been no thorough studies of the delayed fallout
from a nearby explosion beyond the limits of how
the blast, thermal, and direct fallout would affect water flow, soil processes, and ingestion of
radionuclides.  But the ways in which these
stresses would be modified by changes in sunlight
and temperature can only be estimated in the crud-
est fashion.  The total effects may well be far
more serious than would appear from summing estimates for separate sectors of the environment.
This applies to physical, biological, and social
consequences.

## The Overarching Uncertainties

Any resolution of the foregoing problems must
be colored by recognition of the two related uncertainties arching over all the other estimates
and speculations.  For many of the questions there
can be no completely confident judgment in the absence of experimental evidence.  This is true for
the hemispheric dispersion of smoke clouds as well
as the social consequences of impairing soil and
water systems.  Short of a catastrophe, the estimates are bound to remain in the realm of urgent
but poorly grounded speculation.  And a catastrophe, if it were to occur, would likely make
further estimates inconsequential, even if there
were a scientific establishment left to venture
them.

Beyond this lack of verification lies the lack of any knowledge as to whether or not a limited use of nuclear weapons would escalate to a massive exchange. No one can judge with any high probability of correctness, and even if a small probability is admitted as possible, the gravest consequences must be contemplated. We find no comfort in the gaming and strategic analysis that underlies the policy of deterrence or limited strikes. The magnitude of the environmental effects shown in the preceding chapters to be certain, and the consequences of the effects known to be uncertain, leave no room for any policy that permits the possibility of a catastrophic exchange.

## References

Aleksandrov, V. V., and G. L. Stenchikov, 1983: On the modeling of the climate consequences of the nuclear war, Proceedings on Applied Mathematics, Computing Centre of the Academy of Sciences, Moscow.

Budyko, M. I., 1974: Climate and Life, Academic Press, New York and London.

Burton, I., R. W. Kates and G. F. White, 1978: The Environment as Hazard, Oxford University Press, New York.

Coggle, J. E. and P. J. Lindop, 1982: Medical consequences of radiation following a global nuclear war, Ambio, XI, 106-113.

Covey, C., S. H. Schneider and S. L. Thompson, 1984: Global atmospheric effects of massive smoke injections from a nuclear war: results from general circulation model simulations, to be published in Nature.

Crutzen, P. J., and J. W. Birks, 1982: The atmosphere after a nuclear war: twilight at noon, Ambio, XI, 114-125.

Crutzen, P. J., and I. A. Galbally, 1984: Atmospheric effects from post-nuclear fires, to be published in Climatic Change.

Ehrlich, P., C. Sagan, D. Kennedy, and W. O. Roberts, 1984: The Cold and The Dark: The World After Nuclear War, W. W. Norton & Co., New York.

Foley, H. M., and M. A. Ruderman, 1973: Stratospheric NO production from past nuclear explosions, J. Geophys. Res., 78, 4441-4450.

Glasstone, S. and P. J. Dolan, eds., 1977. Effects of Nuclear Weapons, 3rd ed., U.S. De-

partment of Defense and Department of Energy,
Washington, D.C..

Johnston, H. S., G. Whitten, and J. Birks, 1973:
Effects of nuclear explosions on stratospheric nitric oxide and ozone, J. Geophys. Res.,
78, 6107-6135.

Katz, A. M., 1982: Life After Nuclear War - The
Economic and Social Impacts of Nuclear At-
tacks on the United States, Ballinger, New
York.

Kuroda, P. K., U. Miyake and J. Nemoto, 1965:
Strontium isotopes: global circulation after
the Chinese nuclear explosion of 14 May 1965,
Science, 150, 1289-1290.

MacCracken, M. C., 1983: Nuclear war: preliminary estimates of the climatic effects of a
nuclear exchange, presented at the Third
International Conference on Nuclear War,
Erice, Sicily, August.

National Academy of Sciences, 1975: Long-term
Worldwide Effects of Multiple Nuclear-Weapons
Detonations, National Academy of Sciences
Press, Washington,D.C.

Pruppacher, H. R., and J. D. Klett, 1978: Micro-
physics of Clouds and Precipiation, D. Reidel
Publishing Co., Dordrecht, Holland.

Pyle, J. A., and R. G. Derwent, 1980: Possible
ozone reductions and UV changes at the
earth's surface, Nature, 286, 373-375.

Ramanathan, V., and J. A. Coakley, Jr., 1978:
Climate modeling through radiative-convective
models, Rev. Geophys., 16, 465-489.

Schull, W. J., M. Otake, and J. V. Neal, 1981:
Genetic effects of the atomic bombs: a reappraisal, Science, 213, 1220-1227.

Turco, R. P., O. B. Toon, T. Ackerman, J. B.
Pollack and C. Sagan, 1983: Nuclear Winter:
global consequences of multiple nuclear explosions, Science, 222, 1283-1292.

Wetzel, K. G., 1982: Effects on global supplies
of freshwater, Ambio, XI, 126-131.

Williamson, D. L., 1983: Description of NCAR Community Climate Model CCMOB. NCAR Technical
Note TN-210+STR (National Center for Atmospheric Research, Boulder, CO).

World Health Organization (S. Bergstrom et al.)
1983: Effects of a Nuclear War on Health and
Health Services, Report of the International
Committee of Experts in Medical Sciences and
Public Health, WHO Publication A36.12,
Geneva.

Zandecki, A. and S. A. W. Gerstl, 1982: Calcu-
    lations of increased solar UV fluxes and DUV
    doses due to stratospheric ozone depletion,
    Los Alamos National Laboratory, LA-9233-MS.

*Thomas F. Malone*

# 8. What Can the Scientist Do?

## Abstract

Nuclear weapons have evolved from basic theoretical and experimental studies over many decades
that culminated in the demonstration of nuclear
fission in the 1930s, quickly followed by recognition that a chain reaction was possible.
Hiroshima and Nagasaki marked a watershed in the
role of armed conflict as an instrument of the
foreign policy of nations. Both national and
international elements of the scientific community
are becoming increasingly vocal in expressing
their concern and their resolve to fulfill a responsibility which is unique and profound. Quantitative examination of long-term, global effects
of a nuclear exchange severely exacerbate the immediate catastrophic consequences. This new dimension has the potential of illuminating the
hazard to the human species and may well produce
major changes in public attitudes concerning
nuclear warfare. Deep moral and ethical issues
now starkly confront the scientific community.
Dialogue at the international level between the
custodians of scientific knowledge and the custodians of ethics and morality is imperative.

It would be very satisfying if it were possible to propose an overarching, strategical course
of action, persuasive to scientists, that would
enlist their support and hold promise of halting
the seemingly inexorable progress toward a nuclear
war. Unfortunately, there exists no such facile

solution to the question posed by the title of this chapter. There is an analogy here to the answer John von Neumann provided nearly three decades ago to the question he posed in the title of an article he prepared for Fortune magazine (von Neumann, 1955): Can We Survive Technology? After several thousand words, analyzing some of the issues in the incisive manner that might be expected from this remarkable individual, he concluded, "Yes, probably, provided there is a long sequence of small but correct decisions. . .the intelligent exercise of day-to-day judgment." So complex is the problem, and so diverse are scientists in their interests and motivation, that the things scientists can and will do are many and varied. Moreover, they must be pursued persistently over an extended period of time, but with a sense of urgency that grows with the increasing risk of catastrophe.

To contribute to the resolution of one of the most important issues yet to face the human race, the scientist can select from a number of possible roles. The practical difficulty rests with the fact that the issues will be resolved in the political arena by policy makers responsive, in varying degrees in different parts of the world, to popular will. Influencing policy makers directly, or through stimulating popular will, is a task requiring consummate skill if the integrity of the scientific enterprise is to be preserved. Moreover, this is terra incognita to many capable and dedicated scientists.

One course of action, however, would appear to be precluded: to ignore the issue. Nuclear weaponry has its roots deep in developments in science during the past century, and scientists, more than any other group, have a responsibility for the manner in which knowledge generated by the scientific community is used. The issue of nuclear warfare is but one instance of a number of public policy issues which make it imperative that scientists add to their traditional and respected preoccupation with extending knowledge, the dimension of concern for the use to which that knowledge is put. The roots of nuclear weaponry are found in theoretical studies that span the past one hundred years. They can be traced back to the experimental findings of Roentgen on X-rays, of Becquerel and the Curies on radioactivity, and to the theoretical work of Planck on quantum mechanics and Einstein on the Theory of Relativity. Scientific investigations at the famed Cavendish Laboratory in England led in 1932 to Chadwick's discovery of the neutron, first postulated by Rutherford in 1920. The 1920s and 1930s were characterized by intense, worldwide activity. Fermi in Rome, Bohr in Copenhagen, Kurchatov in Leningrad, the Joliot-Curies in France, Nishina and Yukawa in Japan, and Lawrence in Berkeley were among the leaders of a small army of scientists concerned with nuclear physics.

The issue of possible misuse of scientific discoveries surfaced at an early stage. Pierre Curie expressed concern over the possible consequences for humankind of scientists ". . . learning the secrets of nature . . ." in a joint acceptance address at the Nobel Prize ceremonies in 1903. In 1914, H. G. Wells wrote a fictional account of a world run on atomic energy--a world that eventually destroyed itself with an atomic bomb. In his 1920 Bakerian Lecture, Rutherford voiced uneasiness that the energy then well known to be locked in the nucleus of the atom might become accessible ". . . before men had learned to live in peace with their neighbors . . ."

The pace of progress quickened sharply in 1938 with the discovery by Hahn and Strassman that when uranium absorbed a neutron it broke into two lighter atoms. Fission! Frisch and Meitner soon demonstrated that an enormous amount of energy was released in the process. Joliot and his colleagues in France showed that more than one neutron was emitted during fission, thus providing the possibility of a nuclear chain reaction. The scientific basis for nuclear weaponry now existed and word spread rapidly and widely. The Maud Committee in the U.K., charged with examining the military applications of fission, concluded that nuclear weaponry was feasible. The results were communicated to the U.S.; Fermi, Szilard, and their coworkers achieved the first self-sustained nuclear chain at the University of Chicago in 1942. (For details of these historical developments see Bulletin of the Atomic Scientists, 1979; 1982; O'Keefe, 1983.) Alamogordo, Hiroshima, and Nagasaki followed as did, subsequently, the H-bomb and increasingly sophisticated delivery systems for all kinds of nuclear weapons. Pandora's box had been opened!

The implications were savagely clear. For nearly five million years each member of the human species lived with full consciousness that death as an individual awaited him, sooner or later. For the past fifty years, the specter of the extinction of the species has hovered over each of us. Nor will this new condition go away. If we survive for another five million years, we will have learned to live with nuclear weapons. The alternative is not attractive. In essence, the scientist must now confront the ethical and moral issues attendant on his discoveries. This may well involve as complex and tortuous a path as that which led to the discovery of nuclear fission; but this path must be trod. Moreover, coping successfully with this issue will require positive initiatives that present alternatives to the armed conflict rendered obsolete by nuclear weapons. It will be necessary, but not sufficient, to be against war. As discussed by Garfield (1982), science itself is on trial today, great as is our reluctance to admit it. Should we wait for society to turn against science, as more mischievous than beneficial? Or shall we devote to the structuring of a value system for the uses of scientific advances the same commitment we bring to achieving those advances?

What, then, can the scientist do, as the generator, custodian, disseminator, and interpreter of scientific knowledge to contribute to the resolution of this problem--the most important of the present century? There are several things to be done:
- to become informed on the manner in which advances in nuclear physics and missile technology have profoundly and irreversibly altered the nature of conflict;
- to make a commitment to place prevention of nuclear war high on his or her personal agenda;
- to be conscious of the growing awareness that nuclear war is an intrinsically global issue and to participate as vigorously in international efforts to generate knowledge concerning the probable effects of the various scenarios of a nuclear war as did an earlier generation of scientists in

fashioning in all good faith and with great dedication a weapon deemed to be essential for the preservation of a free world--with the added motivation that knowledgeable and scientifically skilled adversaries might possess such a weapon first;

- to share that knowledge widely by individual testimony and to support objective, nonpolitical statements prepared by responsible scientific organizations as a contribution from the scientific community toward an informed public policy;
- to dedicate a specific portion of personal time to the alleviation of some of the tensions and roots of international conflict which, in the contemporary world, have the potential for escalating into nuclear war;
- to be sensitive and responsive to the emerging issues of ethics and morality, and to join with the custodians of those subjects in bringing them into the political decision-making process;
- to participate, as citizens and not as scientists, in the selection of public officials who have an informed and mature perspective on the causes and nature of conflict and an enlightened view of conflict resolution;
- to join with social and behavioral scientists in fashioning instrumentalities for conflict resolution to replace the outmoded resort to military measures;
- to help develop an international consensus on a vision of a better life for all, derived from science, as an alternative to planetary incineration, so that hope for a better future may replace fear of an unacceptable future as the motivation for halting a nuclear arms race that threatens human and spiritual, as well as material, impoverishment in the short term and the possible obliteration of civilization in the long term.

With respect to becoming informed, there is a need to close the generation gap between scientists involved in the original development of nuclear weaponry and the present-day generation. The former were acutely conscious of the potential

155

hazard presented by their handiwork and labored tirelessly to share their concern with others. The latter are all-too-often unaware of the elementary facts--let alone the technological advances that exacerbate the implications of those basic facts. It is important to know, for example, that a medium size H-bomb (10 megatons) has a TNT equivalent six orders of magnitude (a million times) greater than the "block-busters" of World War II that were given that name from the fact that they were capable of devastating an entire city block. The H-bomb is $10^3$ times more powerful than the nuclear weapon used on Hiroshima, and the world's nuclear arsenal is estimated to have $10^6$ times the power of the Hiroshima bomb (the figure of three tons of TNT equivalence for each man, woman, and child on earth is now commonplace knowledge, but bears repeating).

The time required to deliver a nuclear weapon from one continent to another by aircraft has been reduced from somewhat more than ten hours to approximately thirty minutes by missiles with the odds even that it will land within a few hundreds of feet from the target. Airborne vehicles that virtually escape radar detection are already at an advanced stage.

Perhaps one of the best ways for the scientist to be continually informed on nuclear war issues is to read faithfully the authoritative Bulletin of the Atomic Scientists and the publications of the Swedish Institute for Peace Research and those of the Institute of Strategic Studies in London. The eight-volume series Nuclear Weapons Databook being published by the Natural Resources Defense Council will be a rich source of useful information.

Information concerning the immediate impact of a nuclear detonation has been gradually accumulating over the years (see, for instance, Glasstone and Dolan, 1977). As a point of departure it is useful to recall that the blast from a single one Mt weapon would destroy multistory buildings out to a distance of about three miles, killing most people within that radius. Thermal radiation would spontaneously ignite clothing and combustibles out to five miles, with severe damage to frame buildings and second-degree burns to exposed individuals. A ground level detonation would result in lethal radioactive contamination over hundreds of square kilometers, with significant health effects over thousands of square kilometers (Keeny and Panofsky, 1982). The impact of more complex scenarios is discussed by Duffield and von Hipple, chapter 2. Enough is known to be persuasive concerning the unacceptability of using nuclear weaponry, but it is clear that much yet remains to be done in establishing credible data on the immediate effects of a nuclear exchange. Even more pressing is the need to explore intermediate time and distance effects, resulting from atmospheric transport of radioactive debris (Machta, chapter 3).

These are heartening indications that the scientific community is increasingly conscious of its role and responsibility. Statements of concern have been growing in frequency and have recently been taken up by scientific bodies that traditionally have eschewed commenting on matters of public policy. The seminal Russell-Einstein Manifesto (Appendix B), issued in 1955 and signed by an international group of scientists that included seven Nobel Laureates, noted that " . . . a war with H-bombs might quite possibly put an end to the human race . . ." and closed with the thought that "There lies before us, if we choose, continual progress in happiness, knowledge and wisdom. Shall we, instead, choose death, because we cannot forget our quarrels? We appeal, as human beings to human beings: Remember your humanity and forget the rest." This appeal led to convening the first Pugwash Conference on Science and World Affairs that has continued to this day to provide a forum for discussing issues related to nuclear war.

The nongovernmental International Council of Scientific Unions, which counts among its members the scientific communities of seventy countries from all over the world and twenty disciplinary groups (astronomy, physics, chemistry, geophysics and geodesy, etc.), passed a resolution (Appendix C) in 1981 expressing concern over the arms race and urging scientists to extend themselves in emphasizing ". . . the vital necessity of preventing nuclear warfare."

157

At its Annual Meeting in 1982, the National Academy of Sciences passed a resolution (Appendix D) declaring nuclear war ". . . an unprecedented threat to humanity . . ." and calling upon ". . . the President and Congress of the United States and their counterparts in the Soviet Union and other countries which have a similar stake in these matters to intensify efforts to reduce nuclear weapons, to reduce the risk of nuclear war by accident, to inhibit proliferation, to observe arms control agreements and--perhaps most importantly--". . . to avoid military doctrines that treat nuclear weapons as ordinary weapons of war."

The governing bodies of the American Physical Society, the American Association for the Advancement of Science, and the American Meteorological Society have issued unambiguous statements (see Appendices E, F, and G).

Of special interest in the consideration of a nuclear war is the emerging recognition that its effects may well be worldwide and long-term. A preliminary examination (National Academy of Sciences, 1975) drew attention to the depletion of ozone and corresponding increase in ultraviolet radiation as a result of the injection into the stratosphere of a large pulse of oxides of nitrogen released by nuclear detonations. During the decade or so required to replace the ozone by natural processes". . . more or less severe, worldwide effects on climate, crop production, mutagenesis of pathogenic viruses and microorganisms, as well as a marked increase in the incidence of fatally intense sunburn, skin cancer, etc." can be expected. While recovery appeared to be possible, the validity of the findings was limited by the fact that each of these elements was studied independently, without attempting to assess the interactions which would lead to an integrated picture. The need for more research was emphasized repeatedly. The possibility of ". . . irreversible effects on the environment and the ecological system . . ." were acknowledged in a later assessment (Office of Technology Assessment, 1979).

Expressed fears that long-term effects would be global and place in jeopardy human existence were given substance by an assessment under the auspices of the Royal Swedish Academy of Sciences

(Ambio, 1982) of possible human and ecological consequences of a nuclear war. With respect to large-scale and long-term effects, the Advisory Group for the study noted that "One of the conclusions that may be reached from this study is that the short-term effects for which we have relatively reliable calculations--fire, blast and radioactive contamination--may be matched or even vastly overshadowed by longer-term, less predictable environmental effects" (Advisers, 1982). In view of the fact that the study estimated the number of immediate or early deaths would approach 750 million, with another 340 million seriously injured, even this qualified conclusion on large-scale and long-term effects underscores their potential importance. Important new insights emerged from this study regarding the probable effects of loading the atmosphere with strongly light absorbing submicron particles from widespread fires with the possible result of a major reduction in solar radiation. These preliminary findings have been followed by more detailed studies addressing the consequences of a nuclear exchange on the global atmospheric circulation and damaging effects to the delicate ecosystems of which humankind is a part (Turco et al., 1983; Ehrlich et al., 1983).

Clearly, here is an issue urgently in need of illumination by scientists. Why, one may ask, is it desirable to generate new knowledge and assess long-term worldwide effects when the immediate consequences are so horrendous? There are four reasons: First, if it turns out that the lives of everyone everywhere will be placed at risk by a nuclear war, they will rightfully demand a voice in policy decisions on all aspects of nuclear arms. World opinion is likely to be heeded. Second, if a successful "first strike" is suicidal, as surmised by Sagan (1983/84), the whole concept of nuclear war must be re-examined. Third, an international effort will be required to generate the knowledge required for a credible assessment. Conclusions reached by international consensus are more likely to be heeded than are national studies. Finally, if it turns out that the survival of the human race is at stake, the already grave moral issues are elevated to an even higher level.

A mechanism for an international assessment has been established as a result of resolutions passed by the 19th General Assembly of the International Council of Scientific Unions (ICSU) in September 1982, and at the Vth General Assembly of ICSU's Scientific Committee on Problems on the Environment (SCOPE) in June, 1982. The ICSU resolution is as follows:

Recognizing the need for public understanding of the possible consequences of the nuclear arms race and the scientific competence that can be mobilized by ICSU to make an assessment of the biological, medical and physical effects of the large-scale use of nuclear weapons,

Urges the Executive Board to appoint a special committee to study these effects and to prepare a report for wide dissemination that would be an unemotional, non-political, authorizative and readily understandable statement of the effects of nuclear war, even a limited one, on human beings and other parts of the biosphere.

The relevant SCOPE resolution follows:

Considers that the risk of nuclear warfare overshadows all other hazards to humanity and its habitat.

Recommends that the Executive Committee should consider what further action might be appropriate for SCOPE to take.

In view of the SCOPE Resolution, the Executive Board of ICSU referred the matter to SCOPE for action. A preparatory Working Group was convened in London on 10-11 March 1983, under the chairmanship of Sir Frederick Warner, F.R.S. A program was drawn up to assess, through a series of workshops over a two or three year period, the widespread and intense stresses to which a nuclear war would subject ecosystems and the effect on societal systems of the reduced capacity of impacted ecosystems. In effect, the study will examine critically the consequences of several scenarios of a nuclear exchange on the global life support system as defined by Tolba and White (1979).

A steering committee drawn from the scientific communities of France, India, Japan, Sweden, U.K., U.S., and USSR has been appointed. Workshops have been held in Stockholm and New Delhi, and further workshops are planned for Leningrad,

Paris, Budapest, and the U.K. Particular attention is directed toward reducing uncertainties in the dust and soot lofted into the stratosphere for several plausible war scenarios, the consequences of these uncertainties to the atmosphere and climate from these injections, and finally, in the impact of the computed climatic change on the terrestrial and marine biosphere. Since experimental validation is out of the question, it is important that the simulation of consequences be on solid ground.

Although it is hoped that a persuasive assessment can be completed by 1985, it is recognized that what is involved is a sudden perturbation to the chemical, physical, and biological processes that link together the lithosphere, hydrosphere, cryosphere, atmosphere, and biosphere into a closely coupled system capable of combining solar radiation with the biogeochemical cycling of carbon, nitrogen, sulfur, phosphorus, water and other trace nutrients, as well as contaminants to sustain plant, animal, and human life. Particular attention will be paid to the role of the recovery process for the human and environmental system and the interaction between the two, since it is the resiliency of these two systems which will be important in determining the survivability and societal structure for Homo sapiens. It is quite possible that these questions cannot be unambiguously answered without a major international program of research.

It turns out that, quite independently of the issue at hand, there has arisen within the scientific community the conviction that the growth in population and in industrial activity and the intensification of agriculture over the past century have brought society to a stage at which human activity can alter the global life support system over the period of a decade or so. Anthropogenic perturbations to the biogeochemical cycles, and modification of the physical characteristics of the earth's surface by changes in land use, affect the radiant energy which drives the global ecosystem and influences biological productivity which is intertwined with the physical environment by a complex symbiosis, imperfectly understood at the present time. As in the case of the effects of nuclear war, some of these impacts of human activity may be irreversible. Only the time scale for both the impact and recovery are different.

This broader question of global habitability, and the belief that humanity has the potential wisdom and will to plan intelligently its future by prudent management of its environment and natural resources given the body of knowledge required for wise policy choices, led a group of scientists to propose a major research initiative to develop the knowledge base that would make possible preservation of the integrity of the global life support system and insure a sustainable society (see, NASA, 1982).

In connection with the observance of the twenty-fifth anniversary of the International Geophysical Year (IGY) and the twenty-first anniversary of the initiation of the International Biological Program (IBP), the National Academy of Sciences has proposed an International Geosphere-Biosphere Program (IGBP) which would augment and give coherence to the several programs underway in ICSU addressed to the study of the earth's crust and interior, the biosphere, the oceans and atmosphere, and solar terrestrial relations (National Academy of Sciences, 1983).

It is clear that the potential exists for a challenging international, interdisciplinary, scientific investigation that would have its own scientific merit while illuminating the processes that would determine the response of the global life support system to the sudden insult of a nuclear war or the increasing stress of a growing population and a rapidly industrializing society. The prospects for providing the body of knowledge essential to the future well being and prosperity of humanity provide an alternative to the preoccupation of a significant number of scientists and the massive diversion of material resources in the development of improved weaponry that only adds to the overkill capacity of current world nuclear armaments. It is something that scientists can do! Moreover, international cooperation is the kind of confidence-building activity needed to lessen tensions. As D. Gvishiani has pointed out (see Mayor, 1982):

> Global problems make the world aware of the
> need for international cooperation, including
> cooperation in science and technology. By
> its very nature, science is well equipped for
> internationally coordinated efforts directed

to the solution of common problems. Science is universal, independent of nationality, ideological convictions or political orientation, which makes joint efforts much easier than in any other field. Scientists can assess facts rationally and settle disagreements on scientific matters. And if science is to have an influence on global problems, the financial, human and material resources needed are so great that they can only be put together through international cooperation.

A preliminary exploration of an IGBP will be undertaken at a symposium during the General Assembly of ICSU in Ottawa in September 1984. For the immediate future, tensions between East and West pose the gravest threat of a nuclear exchange. For the longer term, it is likely to be exacerbated tensions between the North and South that either directly or indirectly might lead to conflict involving nuclear weaponry.

With respect to East-West tensions, scientists have an important role to play in the manner pointed out by Werner Heisenberg (Heisenberg, 1958):

It is especially one feature of science which makes it more than anything else suited for establishing the first strong connection between different cultural traditions. This is the fact that the ultimate decisions about the value of a special scientific work, about what is correct or wrong in the work, do not depend on any human authority. It may sometimes take many years before one knows the solution of a problem, before one can distinguish between truth and error; but finally the questions will be decided, and the decisions are made not by any group of scientists but by nature itself.

Scientific exchange and collaboration in research have suffered in recent years as a result of increased tension between the U. S. and the Soviet Union. Yet it is precisely when the ideological gap appears to be widest and tensions highest that this channel of communication is particularly needed. A Statement on Science in the International Setting, adopted by the National Science Board at its 238th meeting on 16-17

September 1982, addressed some aspects of this
matter. After remarking that "Scientific cooperation at the international level is an essential
element in the continued vitality of science
. . ." the statement listed scientific cooperation
with industrialized democracies, with developing
countries, and with Communist countries as desirable to maintain the vigor of the U.S. research
efforts. With respect to East-West affairs, the
Board noted that:

> There is also evidence of benefit for U.S.
> science from contacts with scientists from
> Communist countries. Opportunities for indi-
> vidual scientific cooperation, even in the
> presence of strained political relationships,
> keep open channels for communication and can
> lay foundations for enhanced cooperation
> should conditions become more propitious in
> the future. Exchanges with Communist coun-
> tries should be conducted so that commen-
> surate benefits flow to both sides.

Notable examples of East-West cooperation are the
multi-lateral Global Atmospheric Research Program
(GARP) and the highly productive bilateral cooperation on the physics of condensed matter.

Of even more direct bearing on issues of
nuclear war is the initiation and continuation of
bilateral discussions of these matters between designated committees of the Soviet Academy of
Sciences and the U.S. National Academy of
Sciences. It began with a move that Philip
Handler, President of the National Academy of
Sciences, described as ". . . a momentous event in
the history of the Academy." A distinguished
Committee on International Security and Arms Control was established as a vehicle for the National
Academy of Sciences to bring scientific and engineering talent to bear on problems associated with
international security and arms control. Under
the chairmanship of Dr. M. L. Goldberger, President of the California Institute of Technology,
the Committee is to:

- Study and report on scientific and
  technical issues germane to international
  security and arms control;
- Engage in discussion and joint studies
  with like organizations in other
  countries;

• Develop recommendations, statements, conclusions, and other initiatives for presentation to both public and private audiences;
• Expand the interest of U.S. scientists and engineers to international security and arms control; Respond to requests from
• the executive and legislative branches of the U.S. government.

A corresponding group was assembled by the Soviet Academy of Sciences. The quiet dialogue that has ensued in once or twice a year meetings of the two groups serves to illuminate the issues and reflect a meeting of the minds between the scientists from competing nations on their responsibility to leave no stone unturned in seeking to avoid a nuclear war. Topics discussed have included: (1) The necessity of arms control and what negotiations are at the moment most urgent, (2) Questions connected with deep cuts in strategic force levels, (3) Nonproliferation of nuclear weapons, and (4) The consequences of nuclear war, including the problems of limited nuclear war.

A remarkable and promising example of a constructive interaction between Soviet and U.S. scientists took place in connection with the Conference on the World after Nuclear War held in Washington, D.C., 31 October to 1 November 1983 (Ehrlich et al., 1984). Not only was the scientific community of the USSR involved in the preparatory meeting and the Conference itself, but a "Moscow link" was established via satellite so that a live exchange of views took place between a group of scientists in Moscow and a corresponding group in Washington. The dialogue was restricted to scientific issues and agreement was quickly reached that the magnitude of first order effects with respect to a nuclear winter were so large, and the implications so serious, that the issues raised need to be vigorously and critically examined. This examination is proceeding harmoniously in the ICSU/SCOPE project to which reference has been made.

With respect to alleviation of North-South tensions, it has become clear over the past three decades that a strong and vibrant scientific infrastructure within Third World countries is a

necessary, albeit not sufficient, condition for
the economic and social development that would
halt or even reverse the widening gap between
their quality of life and that in the industrialized democracies. Through the activities of the
Board on Science and Technology for International
Development (BOSTID) of the National Academy of
Sciences over two thousand volunteer U.S. scientists and engineers have helped to address the
problems of development in forty developing
nations through (1) study groups that publish
widely-distributed (hundreds of thousands) reports
on the innovative uses of technology, (2) workshops, seminars, and other direct contact with
counterpart groups in those nations, and (3)
giving advice and becoming involved in the BOSTID
research grants program that provides modest assistance to developing country scientists and institutions in support of research and development
on matters vital to their economic growth. There
is a superb and rewarding opportunity to contain
growing tensions by personal involvement in
strengthening of the scientific infrastructure in
developing countries through Academy or university
programs having that objective.

## Ethical and Moral Concerns

The issue of ethics and morality has been
pervasive in discussions of nuclear war, but it
has been elevated to new dimensions over the past
year or so. In 1949, physicist I.I. Rabi warned
that the use of nuclear weapons cannot be justi-
fied on any ethical ground (see, Van Woorst,
1983). Even earlier, Albert Einstein writing in
the Atlantic Monthly for November 1947, said,
"Those to whom the moral teaching of the human
race is entrusted surely have a great duty and a
great opportunity. . . .It is to be hoped that not
only the churches but the schools, the colleges,
and the leading organs of opinion will acquit
themselves well of their unique responsibility in
this regard."

In a letter to Alva Myrdal on 7 March 1978,
Toshiyuki Toyoda, a professor of physics at the
University in Nagoya, Japan, remarked (Bulletin of
the Atomic Scientists, 1979):

I think that disarmament agreements or
treaties should belong to different cate-
gories from other political or economic

166

ones.  Since there is at present no super-
national power which is mandated to exercise
'condign punishment' to violators, any disarmament agreement must have an aspect of
morality, particularly in the present-day
world.

Uneasy over the pace of progress towards
international agreement on the control of nuclear
weaponry and the unmistakable signs that the risk
of nuclear warfare was increasing, a number of
scientists felt in 1981 that the time was propi-
tious to initiate a dialogue between the custodians of scientific knowledge and the custodians
of ethics and morality.  Reverend Theodore M.
Hesburgh, president of the University of Notre
Dame, was consulted and he and Cardinal Franz
Konig, archbishop of Vienna, convened a small
group of scientists in February 1982 to explore
the desirability of a meeting of scientists with
Pope John Paul II, to be followed by discussions
with other religious leaders and scholars of
ethics and morality.  Because the Pontifical Academy of Sciences had already begun discussions
with His Holiness, Professor Carlos Chagas, president of the Pontifical Academy, graciously agreed
to chair the effort.  There was unanimous agreement to proceed and a small drafting group met
subsequently in London to begin preparation of a
declaration to be presented to the Pope.  This was
developed further at a meeting in Rome in June
1982 and a draft document was circulated among a
large group of presidents of academies and other
scientists as a point of departure for discussions
to be held in Rome, 23-24 September 1983.  By co-
incidence, these two dates followed immediately
upon a gathering of academies to observe the bi-
centenary of the "Accademia Nazionale delle
Scienze, called dei XL" which addressed the theme
"The Academies of Sciences towards the Year Two
Thousand."  Following the conclusion of the bi-
centenary symposium many of the group gathered
with a number of other colleagues to complete
drafting the declaration.  This task was completed
24 September and the declaration was formally presented to the Pope by Professor Carlos Chagas
during the course of a visit to the assembled
scientists by His Holiness where he greeted the
members of the conference and thanked them for
their efforts.  It is notable that the final form
of the declaration was approved unanimously (see

167

Appendix H for the text of the declaration)
(Bull. of the Atomic Sci., 1982).

The mood of the occasion was captured by Dr.
Walter Rosenblith, a participant, and foreign
secretary of the National Academy of Sciences, in
his annual report to NAS members:

It is perhaps fair to speculate that those
present not only experienced the uniqueness
of this occasion but may also have been
struck by the collegial spirit of the deli-
berations. The Academies, whose heads were
present, differed in many respects: history,
age, structure, degree of involvement in
studies, research and advisory activities,
relation to governments; they came from different continents, from countries at different stages of development, of different ideo-
logy, etc. The urgent concern for the danger
of nuclear war brought them together.

The declaration noted that the risk is very
great that any utilization of nuclear weapons,
however limited, would escalate to general nuclear
war and in this event there is no prospect that
the mass of the population could be protected, nor
could the devastation of the cultural, economic,
and industrial base of society be prevented. It
remarked that political, economic, ideological,
religious, and all other disputes are small
compared to the hazards of nuclear war. It went
on to declare that "Nuclear warfare would be a
crime acceptance, by all nations of moral principles transcending all other considerations . . ."
It called upon all nations never to be the first
to use nuclear weapons and appealed to national
leaders to eschew military conflict as a means of
resolving disputes. Finally, it appealed to scientists to use their creativity for the betterment
of human life and to religious leaders and other
custodians of moral principles to proclaim forcefully and persistently the grave human issues at
stake.

In a subsequent ecumenical meeting in Vienna
in January 1983, religious leaders joined the call
of the scientists and added their own declaration
of moral and religious convictions. The recent
statement by the Roman Catholic bishops of the
United States, supported by Protestant denomi-

nations and the three branches of Judiasm, is an invitation to probe the ethics of such issues as a deterrence. The Rome Declaration is an indication that scientists are prepared to enter into these discussions which would be crucial to the survival of civilization. An interfaith Academy for Peace has been established at the Ecumenical Institute for Advanced Theological Studies in Jerusalem under the direction of Dr. Landrum Bolling to continue these discussions.

The conclusion cannot be escaped that the era of resolving conflicts and achieving security by military means has come to a close. Alternatives need to be developed. It is heartening, therefore, to note that the International Institute for Applied Systems Analysis has accorded high priority to a project which seeks to improve the negotiation process that will lead to a structured system of negotiations capable of accommodating to the fundamental changes that should take place over the next five years in international security policies and institutions (IIASA, 1983). Participation in this interdisciplinary effort would add the dimension of concern for the consequences of science to the traditional commitment of scientists to extending the frontiers of knowledge.

And so we come to the role of the scientist in presenting to the world a vision of the future as it could be--an alternative to global incineration. It seems clear that our world is at a juncture--a point of transition from which we can envision a set of new and higher, while still quite varied, states of humankind.

Our scientific knowledge--and the capacity to use that knowledge--give us, in principle, a command over energy, matter, life processes, and information handling that enables us to double within decades the per capita capability to transform natural resources into the goods and services necessary to sustain life and give meaning to human existence. In the last decade or so we have become so preoccupied with the recently appreciated negative side--effects of the application of technology--that we have forgotten the tremendous latent potential for good which exists in our scientific capability if we could only learn how to cooperate to exploit it.

Because science has put in the hands of the world the capacity to forge a future better than today, perhaps it is a responsibility of scientists to develop a vision of that future as it could be to hold up against projections of present policies, and to invite dialogue on policy changes that would move the projection nearer to the vision. Effective management of scientific knowledge is an essential ingredient of this progress, and scientists might well accept the challenge to provide the necessary leadership for this effort. If we cannot provide the vision, who will? If not now, when? Plans by the World Resources Institute in Washington, D.C., to sponsor a conference on "Global Possible" in 1984, is a step in the right direction.

The role of the scientist and the destiny of the scientific community were well summarized by Pope John Paul II in a discourse to a gathering of scientists, diplomats, and the Pontifical Academy of Sciences on 12 November 1983, when he remarked that:

> . . . the scientific community is a community of peace, for your rigorous search for truth in the field of nature is independent of ideologies and therefore of the conflicts that result from them . . .

He went on to say:

> The science which brings together those engaged in research, technicians and workers, which mobilizes political and economic power, which transforms society at all levels and in all its institutions, has a task today which is proving more urgent and indispensable than ever before, namely the task of cooperating and building peace . . .

He challenged scientists

> . . . to be united in a common readiness to disarm science and to provide a providential force for peace . . .

## References

Advisers, 1982: Reference scenario: how a nuclear war might be fought, Ambio, XI, 94-99.
Ambio, 1982: Nuclear War: The Aftermath. XI, R. Swedish Academy of Sciences.

Bulletin of the Atomic Scientists, 1979: 35;
1982:38.
Ehrlich, P. R., J. Harte, M. Harwell, P. H. Raven,
C. Sagan, G. M. Woodwell, J. Berry, E. S.
Ayensu, A. H. Ehrlich, T. Eisner, S. J.
Gould, H. D. Grover, R. Herrera, R. M. May,
E. Mayr, C. P. McKay, H. A. Mooney, D.
Pimental, J. M. Teal, 1983: Long-term bio-
logical consequences of nuclear war.
Science, 222, 1293-130.
Garfield, E., 1982: Is public confidence in
science declining?, Current Comments, No. 45,
Institute for Scientific Information.
Glasstone, S. and P. J. Dolan, eds., 1977: Ef-
fects of Nuclear Weapons, 3rd ed., U.S. De-
partment of Defense and Department of Energy,
Washington, D.C..
Heissenberg, W., 1958: Physics and Philosophy--
the Revolution in Modern Science, Vol. XIX,
World Perspectives, Harper & Bros., New York.
International Institute for Applied Systems Ana-
lysis, 1983: Draft of IIASA Research Plan
1984, Luxenburg, Austria.
Keeny, S. K., Jr., and W.K.H. Panofsky, 1982/83:
Mad versus nuts, Foreign Affairs, Winter,
287-304.
Mayor, F., ed., 1982: Scientific Research and
Social Goals, Pergamon Press, New York.
National Academy of Sciences, 1975. Long-term
Worldwide Effects of Multiple Nuclear-Weapons
Detonations, National Academy of Sciences
Press, Washington, D.C.
National Academy of Sciences, 1983: Toward an
International Geosphere-Biosphere Program - A
Study of Global Change, National Academy
Press, Washington, D.C.
National Atmospheric and Space Administration,
1982: Global Change: Impacts on Habitabili-
ty, A Report of the Workshop Held at Woods
Hole, Massachusetts, JPL D-95, Jet Propulsion
Laboratory, California Institute of Techno-
logy, Pasadena, CA.
Sagan, C., 1984: Nuclear war and climatic catas-
trophe: some policy implications, Foreign
Affairs, Winter 83/84, 257-292.
Tolba, M. and G. F. White, 1979: Global Life
Support Systems, United Nations Environment
Programme, Information 47, 5 June 1979,
Nairobi.
Turco, R. P., O. B. Toon, T. Ackerman, J. B.
Pollack and C. Sagan, 1983. Nuclear winter:

global consequences of multiple nuclear explosions, Science, 222:1283-1292.
van Woorst, L. B., 1983: The churches and nuclear deterrence, Foreign Affairs, 61, 827-852.
von Neumann, J., 1955: Can we survive technology?, Fortune, 51, 106-157.

# Appendix A

Resolution Passed by the AAAS Council
(7 January 1982)

## The Catastrophe of Thermonuclear War

Whereas there is worldwide increasing anxiety of the possibility of large-scale nuclear warfare, and

Whereas recent studies have shown that nuclear warfare would inevitably cause death, disease, and human suffering of epidemic proportion without any adequate medical intervention possible, and

Whereas severe trauma to biological and ecological systems would be extended far beyond the immediate bomb impact areas by virture of transport of lethal radioactive debris by air and water, and

Whereas the only effective impediment to such an impending epidemic is the prevention of nuclear warfare,

Therefore be it resolved that the Council of the AAAS support national and international efforts directed toward the prevention of nuclear warfare, and

Be it further resolved that the Council of the AAAS supports Concurrent Resolution 44 which was recently submitted to the United States Senate by Senate Majority Leader Howard Baker of Tennessee. That resolution expresses the conviction of Congress "that the United States Government should not base its policies or weapons programs on the belief that the United States can limit, survive, or win a nuclear war."

Be it further resolved that a symposium be held at the next Annual Meeting on the general subject of "The Effects of Thermonuclear War."

# Appendix B

The Russell-Einstein Manifesto
1955

"In the tragic situation that confronts humanity, we feel that scientists should assemble in conference to appraise the perils that have arisen as a result of the development of weapons of mass destruction . . .

We are speaking on this occasion, not as members of this or that nation, continent or creed, but as human beings, members of the species of Man, whose continued existence is in doubt. The world is full of conflicts; and, overshadowing all minor conflicts, the titanic struggle between Communism and anti-Communism.

Almost everybody who is politically conscious has strong feelings about one or more of these issues; but we want you, if you can, to set aside such feelings and consider yourselves only as members of a biological species which has had a remarkable history, and whose disappearance none of us can desire.

We shall try to say no single word which should appeal to one group rather than another. All, equally, are in peril, and, if the peril is understood, there is hope that they may collectively avert it.

The general public, and even many men in positions of authority, have not realized what would be involved in a war with nuclear bombs. The general public still thinks in terms of the obliteration of cities. It is understood that the new bombs are more powerful than the old, and that, while one A-bomb could obliterate Hiroshima, one H-bomb could obliterate the largest cities, such as London, New York, and Moscow.

No doubt in an H-bomb war great cities would be obliterated. But this is one of the minor disasters that would have to be faced. If everybody in London, New York and Moscow were exterminated, the world might, in the course of a few centuries, recover from the blow. But we now know, especially since the Bikini test, that nuclear bombs can gradually spread destruction over a very much wider area than had been supposed.

It is stated on very good authority that a bomb can now by manufactured which will be 2,500 times as powerful as that which destroyed Hiroshima.

Such a bomb, if exploded near the ground or under water, sends radioactive particles into the upper air. They sink gradually and reach the surface of the earth in the form of a deadly dust or rain. It was this dust which infected the Japanese fishermen and their catch of fish.

No one knows how widely such lethal radioactive particles might be diffused, but the best authorities are unanimous in saying that a war with H-bombs might quite possibly put an end to the human race. It is feared that if many H-bombs are used there will be universal death--sudden only for a minority, but for the majority a slow torture of disease and disintegration.

Many warnings have been uttered by eminent men of science and by authorities in military strategy. None of them will say that the worst results are certain. What they do say is that these results are possible, and no one can be sure that they will not be realized. We have not yet found that the views of experts depend in any degree upon their politics or prejudices. They depend only, so far as our researches have revealed, upon the extend of the particular expert's knowledge. We have found that the men who know most are the most gloomy.

Here, then, is the problem which we present to you, stark and dreadful and inescapable: Shall we put an end to the human race; or shall mankind renounce war? People did not face this alternative because it is so difficult to abolish war.

The abolition of war will demand distasteful limitations of national sovereignty. But what perhaps impedes understanding of the situation more than anything else is that the term mankind feels vague and abstract. People scarcely realize in imagination that the danger is to themselves and their children and their grandchildren, and not only to a dimly apprehended humanity. They can scarcely bring themselves to grasp that they,

175

individually, and those whom they love are in imminent danger of perishing agonizingly. And so they hope that perhaps war may be allowed to continue provided modern weapons are prohibited.

This hope is illusory. Whatever agreements not to use the H-bombs had been reached in time of peace, they would no longer be considered binding in time of war and both side would set to work to manufacture H-bombs as soon as war broke out, for, if one side manufactured the bombs and the other did not, the side that manufactured them would inevitably be victorious.

Although an agreement to renounce nuclear weapons as part of a general reduction of armaments would not afford an ultimate solution, it would serve certain important purposes.

First: Any agreement between East and West is to the good insofar as it tends to diminish tension. Second: The abolition of thermonuclear weapons, if each side believed that the other had carried it out sincerely, would lessen the fear of a sudden attack in the style of Pearl Harbor, which at present keeps both sides in a state of nervous apprehension. We should, therefore, welcome such an agreement, though only as a first step.

Most of us are not neutral in feeling, but, as human beings, we have to remember that, if the issues between East and West are to be decided in any manner that can give any possible satisfaction to anybody, whether Communist or anti-Communist, whether Asian or European or American, whether white or black, then these issues must not be decided by war. We should wish this to be understood, both in the East and in the West.

There lies before us, if we choose, continual progress in happiness, knowledge and wisdom. Shall we, instead, choose death, because we cannot forget our quarrels? We appeal, as human beings, to human beings: Remember your humanity and forget the rest. If you can do so, the way lies open to a new paradise; if you cannot, there lies before you the risk of universal death."

In addition to Albert Einstein and Bertrand Russell, the Manifesto was signed by:

M. Born -- Germany
H. J. Muller -- United States
P. W. Bridgman -- United States
C. F. Powell -- United Kingdom
L. Infeld -- Poland
J. Rotblat -- United Kingdom
F. Joliot-Curie -- France
H. Yukawa -- Japan
L. Pauling -- United States

(From Bulletin of the Atomic Scientists, 1979:<u>35</u>
No. 3, March 14-15)

# Appendix C

International Council of Scientific Unions

Resolution passed unanimously by the ICSU Executive Board at Dubrovnik, Yugoslavia, on 23 September 1981, and approved without dissent by the ICSU General Committee on 25 September 1981.

ICSU:

    - Recalling paragraph 3-a of Part 1 of the Statutes of the Council which says that one of its principal objectives is "to encourage international scientific activity for the benefit of mankind, and so promote the cause of peace and international security throughout the world";

    - Emphasizing that the objectives of the Council, as stated in its Statutes, can be realized only in the atmosphere of peace and stability in the world;

    - Noting the positive effect of efforts to promote mutual understanding and confidence building measures on the development of international scientific cooperation and science as a whole;

    - Expressing concern about recent deterioration of the international situation caused by the continuing arms race;

    - Considering that the scientific community has a special responsibility to initiate actions on a large scale to secure world peace and stability;

    - Urge scientists to do their best to demonstrate to the governments and peoples of all countries the vital necessity of preventing nuclear warfare.

# Appendix D

Resolution of the National Academy of Sciences
(27 April 1982)

Nuclear War and Arms Control

-Whereas nuclear war is an unprecendented threat to humanity;

-Whereas a general nuclear war could kill hundreds of millions and destroy civilization as we know it;

-Whereas any use of nuclear weapons, including use in so-called "limited wars," would very likely escalate to general nuclear war;

-Whereas science offers no prospect of effective defense against nuclear war and mutual destruction;

-Whereas the proliferation of nuclear weapons to additional countries with unstable governments in areas of high tension would substantially increase the risk of nuclear war;

-Whereas there has been no progress for over two years toward achieving limitations and reductions in strategic arms, either through ratification of SALT II or the resumption of negotiation on strategic nuclear arms;

Be it therefore resolved that the National Academy of Sciences calls on the President and the Congress of the United States, and their counterparts in the Soviet Union and other countries which have a similar stake in these vital matters;

-To intensify substantially, without preconditions and with a sense of urgency, efforts to achieve an equitable and verifiable agreement between the United States and the Soviet Union to limit strategic nuclear arms and to reduce significantly the numbers of nuclear weapons and delivery systems;

-To take all practical actions that could reduce the risk of nuclear war by accident or miscalculation;

-To take all practical measures to inhibit the further proliferation of nuclear weapons to additional countries;

-To continue to observe all existing arms control agreements, including SALT II; and

-To avoid military doctrines that treat nuclear explosives as ordinary weapons of war.

# Appendix E

Statement of the American Physical Society
Issued by the APS Council of the American Physical
Society, 23 January 1983

-Whereas nuclear war is an unprecedented threat to humanity;

-Whereas the stockpile of nuclear weapons distributed around the globe contains the explosive power of more than one million Hiroshima bombs;

-Whereas a general nuclear war would kill hundreds of millions of people;

-Whereas the aftereffects of general nuclear war are certain to be catastrophic for the survivors and could destroy civilization;

-Whereas any use of nuclear weapons, including use in so-called "limited wars," would bring with it substantial risk of escalation to general nuclear war:

-Whereas thirty years of vigorous research and development have produced no serious prospect of effective defense against nuclear attack;

-Whereas nuclear arsenals of the United States and the Soviet Union are more than adequate for deterrence;

-Whereas the continuation of the nuclear arms race will not increase the security of either superpower;

-Whereas the proliferation of nuclear weapons to additional countries, especially in areas of high tension, would substantially increase the risk of nuclear war;

-Whereas there has been no progress for several years now toward achieving limitations and reductions in strategic arms, either through ratification of SALT II or the negotiation of a replacement for it;

-Whereas negotiations intended to achieve a comprehensive nuclear test ban have been indefinitely adjourned; and

181

-Whereas negotiations intended to prevent or inhibit the spread of nuclear warfare to outer
space have been suspended;

Be it therefore resolved that The American Physical Society, through its elected Council, calls on
the President and the Congress of the United
States, and their counterparts in the Soviet Union
and other countries which are similarly involved
in these vital matters:

-to intensify substantially, without preconditions
and with a sense of urgency, efforts to
achieve an equitable and verifiable agreement
between the United States and the Soviet
Union to limit Strategic Nuclear Arms and to
reduce significantly the number of such weapons and delivery systems;

-to conduct, in a similar spirit, negotiations to
restrict the use and limit the deployment of
battlefield and intermediate range nuclear
weapons;

-to resume negotiations to prevent the spread of
nuclear weapons to outer space;

-to take all practical measures to inhibit the
further proliferation of nuclear weapons to
additional countries;

-to take all practical actions that would reduce
the risk of nuclear war by accident or miscalculation;

-to continue to observe all existing arms controls
agreements, as well as SALT II;

-to avoid military doctrines and deployments that
treat nuclear explosives as ordinary weapons
of war;

and

-to initiate serious negotiations to ban the testing of nuclear weapons in all environments
for all time as called for in the Non-proliferation Treaty.

# Appendix F

3. <u>International Security, Nuclear War, and
Nuclear Weapons</u>, proposed by the Committee on
Council Affairs (revision of a resolution
drafted by the AAAS Committee on Science, Arms
Control, and National Security, which was
based on a resolution submitted by Herbert L.
Abrams, Clifford A. Barger, William J. H.
Caldicott, Lester Grinspoon, Jerome Gross,
Alexander Leaf, and Mary Ellen Avery):

<u>Whereas</u> reducing tensions between the United
States and the USSR and resolving international disputes short of armed conflict or threat
of nuclear war deserve the highest continued
attention at all levels of our society, and

<u>Whereas</u> the continuation of the nuclear arms
race will not increase the security of either
superpower, and the nuclear arsenals of the
United States and the Soviet Union are more
than enough for deterrence, and

<u>Whereas</u> thirty years of vigorous research and
development have produced no assured prospect
of effective defense against nuclear attack,
and

<u>Whereas</u> (a) there has been no progress for
several years toward achieving limitations and
reductions in strategic arms, either through
ratification of SALT II or the negotiation of
a replacement for it, (b) negotiations intended to achieve a comprehensive nuclear test ban
have been indefinitely adjourned, and (c) negotiations intended to prevent or inhibit the
spread of warfare to outer space have been
suspended,

<u>Be it therefore resolved</u> that the American Associ-
ation for the Advancement of Science urges the
President and the Congress of the United States
and the Government of the Soviet Union:

1. To intensify substantially, without preconditions and with a sense of urgency,
efforts to achieve an equitable and

verifiable agreement between the United States and the Soviet Union to halt the testing, production, and further deployment of nuclear weapons that threaten one another's nuclear deterrent forces, and also to reduce significantly the number of all nuclear weapons and delivery systems.

2. To resume negotiations to prevent the spread of weapons and warfare to outer space.

3. To avoid initiatives toward development of ballistic missile defense (BMD) that are inconsistent with the existing SALT I--Limitations of Anti-Ballistic Missile Systems Treaty.

4. To increase efforts toward greater mutual security through creation of a better climate of international understanding rather than through continuing competition in advanced nuclear weaponry.

# Appendix G

A Statement of the Council
of the American Meteorological Society

30 September 1983

On the Atmospheric Consequences of Nuclear Warfare

Recognizing the inevitable, widespread, devastating consequences of nuclear war by direct explosive effects, and by effects propagated through the atmosphere to the entire globe that could cause the destruction of the biological base that sustains human life, the Council of the American Meteorological Society calls on the nations of the world to take whatever steps are necessary, such as the adoption of appropriate treaties, to prevent the use of nuclear weapons and avoid nuclear war.

# Appendix H

Declaration on Prevention of Nuclear War

Issued 24 September 1982

1. <u>PREAMBLE</u> Throughout its history, human-kind has been confronted with war, but since 1945 the nature of warfare has changed so profoundly that the future of the human race, of generations yet unborn, is imperiled. At the same time, mutual contacts and means of understanding between peoples of the world have been increasing. This is why the yearning for peace is now stronger than ever. Mankind is confronted today with a threat unprecedented in history, arising from the massive and competitive accumulation of nuclear weapons. The existing arsenals, if employed in a major war, could result in the immediate deaths of many hundreds of millions of people, and of untold millions more later through a variety of after-effects. For the first time, it is possible to cause damage on such a catastrophic scale as to wipe out a large part of civilization and to endanger its very survival. The large-scale use of such weapons could trigger major and irreversible ecological and genetic changes, whose limits cannot be predicted.

Science can offer the world no real defense against the consequences of nuclear war. There is no prospect of making defenses sufficiently effective to protect cities since even a single penetrating nuclear weapon can cause massive destruction. There is no prospect that the mass of the population could be protected against a major nuclear attack or that devastation of the cultural, economic and industrial base of society could be prevented. The breakdown of social organization, and the magnitude of casualties, will be so large that no medical system can be expected to cope with more than a minute fraction of the victims.

There are now some 50,000 nuclear weapons, some of which have yields a thousand times greater than the bomb that destroyed Hiroshima. The total explosive content of these weapons is equivalent to a million Hiroshima bombs, which corresponds to a yield of some three tons of TNT for every person on earth. Yet these stockpiles continue to grow.

Moreover, we face the increasing danger that many additional countries will acquire nuclear weapons or develop the capability of producing them.

There is today an almost continuous range of explosive power from the smallest battlefield nuclear weapons to the most destructive megaton warhead. Nuclear weapons are regarded not only as a deterrent, but there are plans for their tactical use and use in a general war under so-called controlled conditions. The immense and increasing stockpiles of nuclear weapons, and their broad dispersal in the armed forces, increase the probability of their being used through accident or miscalculation in times of heightened political or military tension. The risk is very great that any utilization of nuclear weapons, however limited, would escalate to general nuclear war.

The world situation has deteriorated. Mistrust and suspicion between nations have grown. There is a breakdown of serious dialogue between the East and West and between North and South. Serious inequities among nations and within nations, shortsighted national or partisan ambitions, and lust for power are the seeds of conflict which may lead to general and nuclear warfare. The scandal of poverty, hunger, and degradation is in itself becoming an increasing threat to peace. There appears to be a growing fatalistic acceptance that war is inevitable and that wars will be fought with nuclear weapons. In any such war there will be no winners.

Not only the potentialities of nuclear weapons, but also those of chemical, biological and even conventional weapons are increasing by the steady accumulation of new knowledge. It is therefore to be expected that also the means of non-nuclear war, as horrible as they already are, will become more destructive if nothing is done to prevent it. Human wisdom, however, remains comparatively limited, in dramatic contrast with the apparently inexorable growth of the power of destruction. It is the duty of scientists to help prevent the perversion of their achievements and to stress that the future of humankind depends upon the acceptance of all nations of moral principles transcending all other considerations. Recognizing the natural rights of the human race to survive and to live in dignity, science must be

used to assist humankind toward a life of fulfill-
ment and peace.

Considering these overwhelming dangers that
confront all of us, it is the duty of every person
of good will to face this threat. The disputes
that we are concerned with today, including political, economic, ideological and religious ones,
are not to be undervalued but lose their urgency
when compared to the hazards of nuclear war. It
is imperative to reduce distrust and to increase
hope and confidence through a succession of steps
to curb the development, production, testing and
deployment of nuclear weapons systems, and to reduce them to substantially lower levels with the
ultimate hope of their complete elimination.

To avoid wars and to achieve a meaningful
peace, not only the powers of intelligence are
needed, but also the powers of ethics, morality
and conviction.

The catastrophe of nuclear war can and must
be prevented. Leaders and governments have a
great responsibility to fulfill in this regard.
But it is humankind as a whole which must act for
its survival. This is the greatest moral issue
that humanity has ever faced, and there is no time
to be lost.

II. In view of these threats of global nuclear
catastrophe, we declare:

• Nuclear weapons are fundamentally different from conventional weapons. They must not
be regarded as acceptable instruments of warfare.
Nuclear warfare would be a crime against humanity.

• It is of utmost importance that there be
no armed conflict between nuclear powers because
of the danger that nuclear weapons would be used.

• The use of force anywhere as a method of
settling international conflicts entails the risk
of military confrontation of nuclear powers.

• The current arms race increases the risk
of nuclear war. The race must be stopped, the development of new more destructive weapons must be
curbed, and nuclear forces must be reduced, with
the ultimate goal of complete nuclear disarma-

ment.   The sole purpose of nuclear weapons, as long as they exist, must be to deter nuclear war.

III.   Recognizing that excessive conventional forces increase mistrust and could lead to confrontation with the risk of nuclear war, and that all differences and territorial disputes should be resolved by negotiation, arbitration or other peaceful means, we call upon all nations:

• Never to be the first to use nuclear weapons;

• To seek termination of hostilities immediately in the appalling event that nuclear weapons are ever used;

• To abide by the principle that force or the threat of force will not be used against the territorial integrity or political independence of another state;

• To renew and increase efforts to reach verifiable agreements curbing the arms race and reducing the numbers of nuclear weapons and delivery systems.  These agreements should be monitored by the most effective technical means.  Political differences or territorial disputes must not be allowed to interfere with this objective;

• To find more effective ways and means to prevent the further proliferation of nuclear weapons.  The nuclear powers, and in particular the superpowers, have a special obligation to set an example in reducing armaments and to create a climate conducive to non-proliferation.  Moreover, all nations have the duty to prevent the diversion of peaceful uses of nuclear energy to the proliferation of nuclear weapons;

• To take all practical measures that reduce the possibility of nuclear war by accident, miscalculation or irrational action;

• To continue to observe existing arms limitation agreements while seeking to negotiate broader and more effective agreements.

IV.  Finally, we appeal:

•   To national leaders, to take the initiative in seeking steps to reduce the risk of nuclear war, looking beyond narrow concerns for national advantage; and to eschew military conflict as a means of resolving disputes.

•   To scientists, to use their creativity for the betterment of human life and to apply their ingenuity in exploring means of avoiding nuclear war and developing practical methods of arms control.

•   To religious leaders and other custodians of moral principles, to proclaim forcefully and persistently the grave human issues at stake so that these are fully understood and appreciated by society.

•   To people everywhere, to reaffirm their faith in the destiny of humankind, to insist the avoidance of war is a common responsibility, to combat the belief that nuclear conflict is unavoidable, and to labor unceasingly towards insuring the future of generations to come.

Presented to His Holiness the Pope by an assembly of scientists convened by the Pontifical Academy of Sciences

Argentina
A. Stoppani

Austria
K. Komarek
F. König

Belgium
J. Labarbe
J. Peters

Brazil
C. Chagas
M. Peixoto

Bulgaria
A. Balevski
B. Dinkov

Chile
I. Saavedra

Italy
E. Amaldi
F. Benvenuti
E. De Giorgi
G. Marini-Bettolo
R. Levi Montalcini
G. Montalenti
G. Puppi
P. Rossano

Japan
S. Iijima

Korea
T. Shin

Mexico
P. Rudomin

Pakistan
M. Kazi

Czechoslovakia
B. Rysavy

East Germany
W. Kalweit
S. Tannenberger

Egypt
I. Badran

France
P. Jacquinot
J. Lejuene
L. Leprince-Ringuet

Hungary
J. Szentagothai

India
M. Menon

Indonesia
B. Rifai

Ireland
W. Watts

Poland
B. Bilinski
L. Sosnovski

South Africa
E. Simpson

Soviet Union
O. Bykov
S. Isaev
E. Velikhov

Spain
M. Lora-Tamayo

Sweden
C. Bernhard
G. Hambraeus

Taiwan
S. Hsieh

United Kingdom
D. Hodgkin
A. Huxley
A. Porter

United States
D. Baltimore
T. Hesburgh
H. Hiatt
S. Keeny
T. Malone
F. Press
W. Rosenblith
C. Townes
V. Weisskoph

Venezuela
V. Sardi

West Germany
C.F. von Weizäcker

Yugoslavia
J. Sirotkovic

191

# Abbreviated Glossary

Some of the specialized terms and phrases used in current discussions of nuclear war may not be familiar to the general reader. We include a partial list of those terms that are used in this volume. A more complete list is contained in Glasstone and Dolan (1977) from which many of those given here have been taken.

Albedo: The ratio of the amount of energy reflected by a surface to the amount received at the surface, given as a percent.

Alpha particle: A particle emitted spontaneously from the nuclei of some radioactive elements.

Aquifer: A sub-surface stratum of porous and permeable material that can hold and transmit large quantities of water.

Beta particle: A charged particle of very small mass emitted spontaneously from the nuclei of certain radioactive elements. Physically the beta particle is identical to an electron moving at high speed.

Blast Wave (pressure wave): A pulse of air in which the pressure increases sharply at the front. Also called a shock wave.

Chemical Kinetic Rate Coefficient: A measure of the efficiency (rate) with which certain atoms or molecules combine on collision to form other atoms and molecules.

Counterforce Attack: The attack by one side of a confrontation on military installations and missile launch sites of the other side.

Curie: A unit of radioactivity; it is the activity of a quantity of any radioactive species in which $3.7 \times 10^{10}$ nuclear disintegrations occur per second.

Delayed Fallout: See Fallout.

Deterrence: The notion that a stable balance of nuclear weaponry would deter the nuclear powers from waging nuclear war.

Dose: A term denoting the accumulated quantity of ionizing (or nuclear) radiation absorbed by the body.

Dust:   Solid material suspended in the atmos-
        phere in the form of small irregular
        particles many of which are micro-
        scopic in size, radii generally less
        than 10 micron. These particles are
        often of soil substances swept up in
        surface or near surface nuclear ex-
        plosions.
Early Fallout: See Fallout.
Electromagnetic Pulse (EMP):   A sharp pulse
        of electromagnetic radiation in the
        long-wavelength  (radio  frequency)
        range.
Energy Yield (Equivalent Energy Yield):   The
        total effective energy released in a
        nuclear explosion.  It is usually
        expressed in terms of the equivalent
        tonnage of TNT required to produce
        the same energy released in an ex-
        plosion.
Fallout:   In this context it is the process
        or phenomenon of settling to the
        earth's surface of solid particles
        contaminated  with  radioactive
        material from the radioactive cloud;
        Early (Local) Fallout:  Radioactive
        substances, generally larger than
        100 microns, that reach the earth
        within about 24 hours after a nucle-
        ar explosion; Delayed (Worldwide)
        Fallout:  Smaller contaminated par-
        ticles that are transported globally
        and brought to earth over extended
        periods  ranging  from  months  to
        years.
Fission:   The process whereby the nucleus of
        a particular heavy chemical element
        splits into (generally) two nuclei
        of lighter elements, with the re-
        lease of substantial amounts of en-
        ergy.
Fusion:   The process whereby the nuclei of
        light chemical elements, especially
        those of the isotopes of hydrogen,
        combine to form the nucleus of a
        heavier element with the release of
        substantial amounts of energy.
Gamma Radiation:   Electromagnetic radiation
        of high photon energy atwavelengths
        less than 0.1 nanometers originating

in atomic nuclei and accompanying many nuclear reactions.

Gray (Gy): A unit of ionizing (or nuclear) radiation absorbed by the body. It corresponds to the energy absorption of 1 joule per kilogram of tissue. 1 Gy = 100 rads.

Half-life: The time required for the activity of a given radioactive to decrease to half of its initial value due to radioactive decay.

Ionizing Radiation (See, also, Nuclear Radiation): Electromagnetic radiation (gamma rays or X-rays) or particulate radiation (alpha particles, beta particles, neutrons, etc.) capable of producing ions, i.e., electrically charged particles, directly or indirectly, in its passage through matter.

Isotopes: Forms of the same elements having identical chemical properties but differing in their atomic masses (due to different numbers of neutrons in their respective nuclei) and in their nuclear properties.

Megaton (TNT) (see Energy Yield): Defined strictly as $4.2 \times 10^{15}$ joules. This is approximately the amount of energy that would be released by the explosion of a million tons of TNT.

$NO_x$: Oxides of nitrogen (NO and $NO_2$).

Nuclear Radiation (See, also, Ionizing Radiation): Particulate and electromagnetic radiation emitted from atomic nuclei in various nuclear processes. All nuclear radiations are ionizing radiations.

Nuclear Weapon: A general name given to any weapon in which the explosion results from the energy released by reactions involving atomic nuclei, either fission or fusion or both.

Overpressure (see Blast Wave): The transient pressure usually expressed as pounds per square inch (psi), exceeding the ambient pressure, manifested in the shock (or blast) wave from an explosion.

194

Ozone layer: That part of the atmosphere in which the ozone concentration is the greatest - generally 15-30 kilometers.

Person Sievert: See Sievert.

Pressure Wave: See Blast Wave.

Psi: The unit commonly used to express over-pressure as a result of a blast or shock wave emanating from an explosion. One psi = 0.0689 bars = 68.9 mb.

Rad (Roentgen Absorbed Dose): A unit of absorbed dose of radiation. It is equal to $10^{-2}$ joules of nuclear (or ionizing) radiation per kilogram of absorbing body tissue (i.e. 1 rad = $10^{-2}$ gray).

Radioactivity: The spontaneous emission of radiation, generally alpha or beta particles, often accompanied by gamma rays, from the nuclei of an unstable isotope.

Radionuclide: A radioactive atomic species.

Rem: A unit of biological dose of radiation derived from the initial letters of the term "roentgen equivalent mammal". The numbers of rems of radiation is equal to the number of rads absorbed multiplied by the relative biologically effectiveness of the given radiation.

Residence Time: In the present context it is the time required for the amount of radioactive debris deposited in a particular part of the atmosphere to decrease to half of its initial value.

Roentgen (R): A unit of exposure to gamma (or X-ray) radiation. An exposure of one roentgen is approximately equal to an absorbed dose of one rad in soft body tissue.

Sievert (Sv): A unit of dose equivalent equal to one joule per kilogram. One Sv is the radiation dose equivalent in biological effectiveness to one Gy of gamma radiation. 1 Sv = 100 rems. A person-Sv is a unit expressing the collective dose to a population.

Smoke: Airborne particulate matter resulting from various combustion processes.

Soot: Airborne particulates, primarily elemental carbon, resulting from combustion processes from forest fires and other carbonacious material.

Strategic Weapon (see Tactical Weapon): Nuclear weapons that have long ranges and large energy yields (generally ballistic missiles).

Stratosphere: A thermally stable layer in the atmosphere where the temperature is nearly constant or increases with height. The base of the stratosphere varies from about 18 kilometers at the equator to about 8 kilometers near the poles. The top of the stratosphere is at about 50 kilometers. The stratosphere is characterized by a long residence time for dust, smoke, and radioactive debris.

Tactical Weapons: Weapons that generally have a small range (less than a few hundred kilometers) and relatively small equivalent energy yield (less than a few thousand tons of TNT).

Tropopause: The boundary between the troposphere and the stratosphere at which there is usually an abrupt change in temperature lapse rate. In midlatitudes the tropopause is often indistinct and could represent a boundary about 2-3 kilometers thick.

Troposphere: That portion of the earth's atmosphere from the surface to the tropopause. The troposphere is the atmospheric region where most "weather" occurs. It is characterized by a decreasing temperature with height, large scale vertical mixing and clouds and precipitation.

UV-B: The integrated ultraviolet radiation in the wavelength interval 0.28 to 0.32 microns. This radiation is biologically damaging to plants and animals.

Vadose Zone: The unsaturated zone above the water table and through which surface water percolates downward.

X-rays: High energy electromagnetic radiation in the wavelength interval 0.1 to 10 nanometers.

# Selected Bibliography

Adams, R. & S. Cullan, eds., 1981: The Final Epidemic, Bulletin of the Atomic Scientists, Chicago, 1981.

Annenkov, B. N., I. K. Dibobes, and R. M. Aleksakin, eds., 1973: Radiobiology and Radioecology of Farm Animals, U.S. Atomic Energy Commission Technical Information Center, Oak Ridge, TN.

Ayers, R. N., 1965: Environmental Effects of Nuclear Weapons, 3 vols., Hudson Institute, Croton-on-Hudson, New York.

Barnaby, F. B., J. Rotblat, H. Rodhe, L. Kristoferson, J. Prawitz, and J. Peterson, 1982: Reference scenario: how a nuclear war might be fought. Ambio 2-3, 94-99.

Bensen, D. and A. Sparrow, eds., 1971: Survival of Food Crops and Livestock in the Event of Nuclear War, U.S. Atomic Energy Commission, Washington, D.C.

Bolt, B., 1976: Nuclear Explosions and Earthquakes: The Parted Veil, W.H. Freeman and Co., San Francisco.

British Medical Association, 1983: The Medical Effects of Nuclear War, London.

Bunn, Mathew and Kosta Tsipisk, 1983: The Uncertainties of a Preemptive Nuclear Attack, Sci. Amer., 249, 38-47.

Chandler, C.C., et al., 1963: Prediction of fire spread following nuclear explosion. U.S. Forest Service Res. Pap. PSW-5. Pacific Southwest Forest Range Experiment Station, Berkeley, CA.

Chazov, E., L. A. Ilyin and A. K. Gushkova, 1982: The Danger of Nuclear War, Novosti Press, Moscow.

Chivian, E., ed., 1982: Last Aid: The Medical Dimensions of Nuclear War, International Physicians for the Prevention of Nuclear War, W. H. Freemanand Co., San Francisco.

Drell, S. D. and F. von Hippel, 1976: Limited Nuclear War, Sci. Amer. 235, 27-37.

Ehrlich, P. R., E. S. Ayensu, J. Berry, T. Eisner, S. J. Gould, H. D. Grover, J. Harte, M. Harwell, R. Herrera, R. M. May, E. Mayr, C. P. McKay, H. A. Mooney, D. Pimental, P. H. Raven, C. Sagan, J. M. Teal, and G. M. Woodwell, 1983: Long-term biological consequences of nuclear war. Science, 222, 1293-130.

Fetter, S. and K. Tsipis, 1981: Catastrophic re-
    leases of radioactivity, Sci. Amer. <u>244</u>,
    41-47.
Glasstone, S. and P. J. Dolan, eds., 1977: <u>Ef-
    fects of Nuclear Weapons</u>, 3rd ed., U.S.
    Department of Defense and Department of
    Energy, Washington, D.C..
Greene, O., other authors, 1982: <u>London After the
    Bomb</u>, Oxford University Press, London.
Ingersoll, Andrew P., 1983: The Atmosphere, Sci.
    Amer., <u>249</u>, 162-174.
Ishikawa, E. and D. Swain, eds., 1981: Committee
    for the Compilation of Materials on Damage
    Caused by the Atomic Bombs in Hiroshima and
    Nagasaki. <u>Hiroshima and Nagasaki: The Phys-
    ical, Medical, and Social Effects of the
    Atomic Bombings</u>, Basic Books, New York.
Katz, A. M., 1979: <u>Economic and Social Conse-
    quences of Nuclear Attacks on the United
    States</u>, Report to Committee on Banking,
    Housing, and Urban Affairs, U.S. Senate,
    Washington, D.C.
Katz, A. M., 1982: <u>Life After Nuclear War -- The
    Economic and Social Impacts of Nuclear
    Attacks on the United States</u>, Ballinger, New
    York.
Lavrenchik, V., 1965: <u>Global Fallout Products of
    Nuclear Explosions</u>, Atomizdat, Moscow,
    AEC-tr-6666.
Lewis, K., 1979: The prompt and delayed effects
    of nuclear war, Sci. Amer. <u>241</u>, 35-47.
National Academy of Sciences, 1975: <u>Long-term
    Worldwide Effects of Multiple Nuclear-Weapons
    Detonations</u>, National Academy of Sciences
    Press, Washington, D.C.
National Academy of Sciences, 1980: <u>The Effects
    on Populations of Exposure to Low Levels of
    Ionizing Radiation</u>, (BEIR III) National Acad-
    emy of Sciences Press, Washington, D.C.
National Academy of Sciences, 1982: <u>Causes and
    Effects of Stratospheric Ozone Reduction: An
    Update</u>, National Academy of Sciences Press,
    Washington, D.C.
National Academy of Sciences, 1984: <u>Report of the
    Committee on Atmospheric Effects of Nuclear
    Explosions</u>, National Academy of Sciences
    Press, Washington, D.C.
Polikarpov, G. G., 1966: <u>Radioecology of Aquatic
    Organisms</u>, translated by Scripta Technica,
    Ltd., Reinhold Book Div., New York.

Rotblat, J., 1981: <u>Nuclear Radiation in Warfare</u>, Stockholm International Peace Research Institute, Stockholm.

Sagan, C., 1984: Nuclear war and climatic catastrophe: some policy implications, Foreign affairs, Winter 83/84, 257-292.

Schell, J., 1982: <u>The Fate of the Earth</u>, Alfred Knopf, New York.

Turco, R. P., O. B. Toon, T. Ackerman, J. B. Pollack and C. Sagan, 1983: Nuclear Winter: global consequences of multiple nuclear explosions, Science, <u>222</u>, 1283-1292.

United Nations (U.N.), 1981: <u>Comprehensive Study on Nuclear Weapons</u>, Report of the Secretary General, New York.

U.N., Scientific Committee of U.N. on Effects of Atomic Radiation, 1982: <u>U.N. Document A/AC/82/G/L</u>.

U.N., 1979: <u>The Effects of Weapons on Ecosystems</u>, United Nations Environmental Programme, Nairobi.

Upton, Arthur C., 1982: The Biological Effects of Low-level Ionizing Radiation, Sci. Amer., <u>246</u>, 41-49.

U.S., Arms Control and Disarmament Agency, 1979: <u>The Effects of Nuclear War</u>, Government Printing Office, Washington, D.C.

U.S. Congress, Office of Technology Assessment, 1979: <u>The Effects of Nuclear War</u>, U.S. Congress, Office of Technology Assessment.

U.S. Congress, 1982: <u>The Consequences of Nuclear War on the Global Environment</u>, Hearing before Committee on Science and Technology, U.S. House of Representatives, Government Printing Office.

U.S. Department of Agriculture, 1962, <u>Soil, Crops, and Fallout from Nuclear Attack</u>, U.S. Department of Agriculture, Washington, D.C.

U.S. Department of Agriculture, 1964: <u>The Effect of Radioactive Fallout on Soils and Plants</u>, USSR, U.S. Department of Commerce, Office of Technical Services, Washington, D.C.

Westing, A. H., 1980: <u>Warfare in a Fragile World: Military Impact on the Human Environment</u>, Taylor & Francis (SIPRI), London.

Woodwell, G. M., ed., 1963: <u>The Ecological Effect of Nuclear War</u>, Brookhaven National Library, Stony Brook, NY.

World Health Organization (S. Bergstrom et al.) 1983: <u>Effects of a Nuclear War on Health and Health Services</u>, Report of the International

Committee of Experts in Medical Sciences and
Public Health, WHO Publication A36.12,
Geneva.
York, Herbert F., 1983: Bilateral Negotiations
and the Arms Race, Sci. Amer. 249, 149-160.
Zuckerman, S., 1982: Nuclear Illusion and
Reality, Viking Press, New York.

# About the Authors

Julius S. Chang is Director of the Regional Acid Deposition Modeling Project at the National Center for Atmospheric Research, P. O. Box 3000, Boulder, Colorado 80307. He received a Ph.D. in applied mathematics and statistics from the State University of New York, Stony Brook. As a staff member of the Lawrence Livermore National Laboratory (1972-1983) he was involved in research on the transportation and transformation of chemicals in the atmosphere. He has been active in international reviews of ozone problems, and co-edited with M. C. MacCracken at Lawrence Livermore a 1975 preliminary study of potential climate and chemical effects of atmospheric nuclear explosions.

John Duffield is a graduate student in the Woodrow Wilson School of Public and International Affairs at Princeton University, Princeton, New Jersey, 08544. He was a research associate in Princeton University's Center for Energy and Environmental Studies.

Frank von Hippel is a senior research physicist at the Center for Energy and Environment Studies, Princeton University, Princeton, New Jersey 08544. He holds a Ph.D. in theoretical physics from Oxford University. His research has dealt with elementary particle physics; with problems of energy policy including reactor safety and urban and military technologies; and with the consequences of limited nuclear war. He is chairman of the Federation of American Scientists, and is co-author of Advice and Dissent: Scientists in the Political Arena (1974).

Julius London is Professor of Astrophysical, Planetary and Atmospheric Sciences at the University of Colorado, Boulder, Colorado 80309. He received a Ph.D. in Meteorology from New York University. He is past president of the International Radiation Commission (IAMAP). His research interests have involved studies of the earth's radiation budget and its relation to climatic change. He was, with Gilbert White, co-organizer of the AAAS symposium on The Environmental Effects of Thermonuclear War.

Lester Machta is Director, Air Resources Laboratories, Environmental Research Laboratories,

the National Oceanic and Atmospheric Administration, Rockville, Maryland 20852. He holds an
Sc.D. in meteorology from Massachusetts Institute
of Technology. His research with the Weather
Bureau and its successor agencies has dealt with
local and global aspects of the meteorology of air
pollution. He has participated in numerous
national, United Nations, and World Meteorological
Organization activities related to problems of
pollution in the atmosphere including the Geneva
Test Ban Conference and the United Nations Scientific Committee on the Effects of Atomic Radiation.

Thomas F. Malone is a senior consultant with
Resources for the Future, 1755 Massachusetts Ave.,
N.W., Washington, D.C. 20036. He holds an Sc.D.
from Massachusetts Institute of Technology in
meteorology. While director of the Holcomb Research Institute, Butler University (1973-1983) he
was deeply involved in national and international
studies of atmospheric problems, and as Foreign
Secretary of the National Academy of Sciences
(1978-1982) he stimulated many international
scientific enterprises. He is treasurer of the
International Council of Scientific Unions, and
represents it on the SCOPE Steering Committee on
Environmental Effects of Nuclear War.

Arthur C. Upton is Director of the Institute
of Environmental Medicine, New York University
Medical Center, New York, New York 10016. He
holds an M.D. from the University of Michigan.
His research as a pathologist at the State University of New York, Stony Brook, and at Brookhaven
National Laboratory (1954-1975) was, in part, on
the relation of radiation injury to endocrine
functions and to cancer. He is the author of
Radiation Injury: Effects, Principles and
Perspectives (1969).

Gilbert F. White is Gustavson Distinguished
Professor Emeritus of Geography at the Institute
of Behavioral Science, the University of Colorado
at Boulder, Colorado 80309. He holds a Ph.D. in
geography from the University of Chicago. He
jointly edited a report of the United Nations
Environment Programme on The World Environment,
1972-1982 and is director of the Natural Hazards
Research Applications and Information Center. He
is a member of the Steering Committee of the SCOPE

project on the Environmental Effects of Nuclear War.

George M. Woodwell is Director of the Ecosystems Center of the Marine Biological Laboratory, Woods Hole, Massachusetts 02543. He holds a Ph.D. in ecology from Duke University. As senior scientist at the Brookhaven National Laboratory (1965-1975), he launched a series of studies on the effects of ionizing radiation and toxic substances on the structure and functions of terrestrial ecosystems. He edited the 1963 report on Ecological Effects of Nuclear War and in 1984 the SCOPE report on global stocks of terrestrial carbon. He chaired the 1983 Conference on the World After Nuclear War.

Donald J. Wuebbles is a member of the scientific staff of the Lawrence Livermore National Laboratory, Livermore, California 94550. He received his Ph.D. in atmospheric sciences from the University of California, Berkeley. His research is concerned with human impacts on climate and with the chemistry and numerical modeling of atmospheric processes.

# Acknowledgment

The editors would like to express their appreciation to Mary S. Sable for major editorial assistance in preparation of the manuscripts for this volume.